Security, Strategy and the Global Economics of Defence Production

D1605677

The Canada-United Kingdom Colloquia Series

The Communications Revolution at Work: The Social, Economic and Political Impacts of Technological Change, Robert Boyce, editor

Security, Strategy and the Global Economics of Defence Production, David G. Haglund and S. Neil MacFarlane, editors

Security, Strategy and the Global Economics of Defence Production

Edited by David G. Haglund
and S. Neil MacFarlane

Published for the School of Policy Studies, Queen's University
by McGill-Queen's University Press
Montreal & Kingston • London • Ithaca

Canadian Cataloguing in Publication Data

Main entry under title:

Security, strategy and the global economics of defence production

(The Canada-United Kingdom colloquia series)
Proceedings of the Canada-UK Colloquium held Nov. 5-8, 1998, Halifax,
N.S.
Includes bibliographical references
ISBN 0-88911-877-9 (bound)
ISBN 0-88911-875-2 (pbk.)

1. Defense industries – Canada – Congresses. 2. Defense industries – Great
Britain – Congresses. 3. National security – Canada – Congresses.
4. National security – Great Britain – Congresses. I. Haglund, David G.
II. MacFarlane, S. N. (Stephen Neil), 1954-   . III. Queen's University
(Kingston, Ont.). School of Policy Studies. IV. Canada-UK Colloquium
(1998 : Halifax, N.S.). V. Series.

HD9743.C22S42 1999   338.4'76233'0971   C99-931925-6

Contents

Foreword

Rear-Admiral D.E. "Dusty" Miller

I

It is a great privilege for me to be able to contribute a Foreword to this volume on Canadian-British defence issues. Military cooperation between our two countries is a subject very dear to my heart, and indeed reflects my past posting as the Commander of the Canadian Defence Liaison Staff in London from 1995 to 1997. During that time I worked with colleagues at the High Commission to formulate the text of the joint declaration concerning Canada-UK relations, signed by our prime ministers at the Denver G7 summit on 30 June 1997.

As High Commissioner Roy MacLaren often stated, "scratch any British person and you will find a tie to Canada." Some 30 percent of Canadians regard themselves as being of British origin, and I am one of their number.

My grandfather served in the Canadian Army during World War I. He lived in Winnipeg and went to war as a member of the Royal Winnipeg Engineers. He suffered shell shock badly and was told by doctors in Winnipeg following the conflict that he would have only six months to live if he stayed in the harsh Manitoba climate — a little longer if he packed up his four children and moved to a more temperate clime such as that of the UK, his original homeland. So he moved. As he grew older he lost a bit of hearing, and loud noises no longer bothered him — and he lived on, outlasting all six of the doctors who had predicted how little time he had left. He finally died at age 97, after getting to know my own children, his great-grandchildren, when I was attending the Royal Naval Staff College in 1978-79.

My father was an officer in the Royal Air Force during World War II when my mother met him. Her brother, my uncle, was at D-Day + 2 — Canadian born, but in the Royal Signals Regiment. Scratch any Canadian....

In 1914 and 1939 Canada was the first of Britain's dominions to come to its support. Troops from all across the country, as well as from Newfoundland which joined Confederation in 1949, shared fully in the tragedies and victories of both wars. On the battlefield — Vimy Ridge, Dieppe, D-Day landings — and off the battlefield (in factories, shipyards, farms, and hospitals; and from their savings) Canadians made superhuman efforts to support Britain. In cities and towns in *both* countries stand monuments to this joint sacrifice. As a member of the Commonwealth War Graves Commission during my time in the UK, I came to appreciate several monuments first hand. My favourites were Brookwood Cemetery southwest of London where some 3,000 Canadians from both wars are buried. On 11 November 1995 we stood among those graves for the ceremony with the Canada-UK Veterans Association. My wife found her cousin, who had fought in the Royal Canadian Air Force (RCAF), buried there. Her father flew a Spitfire during the war, and was also in the RCAF. Yes, our ties do run deep.

In Folkestone Cemetery, on England's south coast, there has been a tribute every year since 1919 to the 300 Canadians who lie buried there. The tribute takes place every Canada Day, 1 July. Students from the 12 local schools place homemade posies on each Canadian's grave. Such gestures bind us together in memory of those we have lost and in recognition of the preciousness of our shared democratic values.

I found it fascinating that 30,000 Canadian troops trained for the D-Day landings at Inverary, Scotland. There now exists a fine Canadian section in the museum at Inverary, commemorating this particular contribution.

I could go on, but shall conclude this introductory portion of the Foreword by referring to the unique Canadian contribution to the Battle of the Atlantic. Canadians built 123 *Flower* class corvettes, which turned the tide by mid-1943 and got the upper hand on the dreaded threat to our valiant merchant mariners. The very last corvette, *HMCS Sackville*, is restored and proudly sits in our harbour as our official naval memorial. Also not to be forgotten is the humble and moving Canadian memorial in Green Park, next to Canada Gate at Buckingham Palace: two triangular monuments pointing directly at Halifax, whence that tremendous war effort left.

II

When I returned from the UK rather abruptly to the next best job a naval officer could ever have, I met with our Chief of Defence Staff to discuss who my relief would be. With pressures on him both to "downsize" and "downrank," he wanted to know what I thought of reducing the rank of the CDLS(L) military head. I replied, "not much!"

Consider the following. The UK sends 12,000 soldiers a year to CFB Suffield to be trained at the brigade level, a large undertaking, very much appreciated as well as a model of Canada-UK military cooperation. The Royal Air Force trains in low-level flying at Goose Bay, Labrador. NATO Flying Training in Canada (NFTC) is a major future project, for which we have the space to collaborate and to make pilot training economical and efficient for the alliance. The UK has agreed in principle to commit to the training. The British Aerospace Hawk has been chosen by Canada to be the training aircraft. Suffice it to say with NFTC, submarines, and major helicopter projects, the time was hardly propitious to downrank our military representation; nor would such an action have been appropriate.

The Denver agreement specifically mentioned military exchanges, in a passage indicating that "consideration will be given to enhancing bilateral military cooperation both at the policy level, especially in NATO fora, and in the area of military-to-military contacts, including defence procurement and exercises; and to maintaining the level of military exchanges." Regimental exchanges had been at the core of our continued cooperation and military relationship for years. We have almost lost them despite our best efforts. I would like to see them restored and increased. Exchanges cost very little, as they are reciprocated on a one-for-one basis. Reversing the recent, worrisome trend toward their obliteration makes sense, and should be done.

The reopening of Canada House on Trafalgar Square by Her Majesty Queen Elizabeth was a great event. For the first time since the 1950s the Canadian military provided the guard at Buckingham Palace and PPCLI made us proud. In May 1998 *HMCS Fredericton* displayed one of our new frigates to downtown London. We have introduced 28 new ships into our Navy since the Gulf War in 1991. We have gone from a steam-driven Navy to a super-microchip computerized Navy with totally Canadian technology and design. Our 1,000-ton coastal defence vessels take containerized packages for mine-hunting and -sweeping, route survey, remote operating vehicles, and deep-sea investigation submersibles — the latter of which proved their worth in the Swissair disaster.

We have the best capability in the world to map the ocean floor and to superimpose computer programs onto the mapping for a three-dimensional representation. Moreover:

- our frigates' computer systems are totally operational each with more power than a US *Aegis* cruiser;

- the Canadian helicopter hauldown system has been sold to several countries, including the United States, and the Royal Navy knows this Canadian system would increase its operational capability; and

- our coastal defence vessels are multi-purpose and represent our best current high-tech investment.

Today we have a ship in STANAVFORLANT — *HMCS Montreal*, working alongside *HMS Lancaster*. We took command of SNFL in April 1999, for the millennium year. *HMCS St. John's* is with SNFORMED and was in the Adriatic alongside *HMS Cardiff* during the autumn 1998 crisis in Kosovo. In Bosnia we still have some 1,200 troops serving alongside British counterparts. And, of course, in the fighting against Serbia, Canadian pilots have been alongside their British and other allied counterparts.

At present we have two maritime patrol aircraft in Lossiemouth, participating in the Royal Navy's joint maritime course. This is a regular occurrence. Moreover, our ships still operate together in the Persian Gulf. Indeed it was *HMS Gloucester* that led *Athabaskan*, my command ship, through the Suez Canal in 1990.

The above paragraphs provide some indication of the nature and extent of Canada-UK military cooperation today. What of the future framework of that cooperative relationship? The opportunities are numerous and exciting.

III

I begin here with the *Upholder* submarines. Their purchase constitutes a tremendous opportunity to keep our long-term submarine association alive. *Oberon* training, including sea training, along with the *Upholders* will begin in the UK and will move to Canada. Trainers will be in Halifax with a full-term presence of one submarine on our west coast.

NATO Flying Training in Canada provides another venue for bilateral cooperation. As I noted above, Bombardier, our Canadian contractor, has chosen the BAe Hawk to be the training aircraft for NATO pilots. We look forward to a positive RAF commitment to train in Moose Jaw, at a more economical cost than if any one country attempted training alone.

In Bosnia our regiments have bonded together during real-time operations; there is no substitute for this. This will keep our armies mutually respectful for at least a decade. But we must build on this experience. Without such exposure, military exchanges become critical, not just nice to have.

Equipment needs of the Canadian Forces can provide yet another avenue for future bilateral cooperation. Canada needs new maritime helicopters. We currently fly some 35 Sea Kings celebrating their thirty-fifth anniversary. They represent 1950s technology flying on and off ships equipped with twenty-first-century technology. The process of replacing them needs speeding up. The Westland/Agusta EH-101 Cormorants were chosen to replace our Labrador search and rescue helicopters. Our Navy's top priority is to obtain a capable Sea King replacement.

As well, we have on the drawing board a type of command-and-control logistic sealift capability, needed to replace our present replenishment ships.

The United Kingdom is a leading exporter of defence products, ranking at or near the top once the United States, which dominates world markets, is factored out of the equation. As such, UK industry presents important opportunities for collaboration.

The UK's aerospace industry is a major global player, with turnover in the order of $20 billion (split fairly evenly between the civil and military sectors); this is roughly 10 percent of the world aerospace market. Of this portion, some 60 percent is exported. Again, these figures underline the fact that the opportunities presented through collaboration with UK industry are not restricted to the domestic market.

In spite of the downward trend in the UK defence budget, Canadian suppliers of defence and aerospace equipment have managed to increase their exports to Britain over the past few years. From a total of $331 million in 1993, these rose to $377 million in 1994, and to $476 million in 1995. Canadian imports from the UK of these same product groups were equally impressive, thus confirming the broad and closely integrated relationship to be found between the British and Canadian aerospace and defence industries.

In respect of market trends, the UK Ministry of Defence (MOD) is moving from procuring complete platforms (e.g., new aircraft or ships) toward improving its capabilities regarding weapons and sensors, and the electronic integration of these two groups. Canadian firms have enjoyed recent export successes in a number of related areas, notably sonar and radar systems, space and tactical communications systems, and targeting systems. These successes have in part stemmed from MOD's policy to buy "commercial, off-the-shelf" whenever possible, in order to reduce costs. The cost of training has also pushed the MOD toward simulation in all areas, resulting in some notable successes for Canada in the area of flight-simulation equipment.

Nor is defence cooperation simply an intergovernmental affair; private industry has a huge role to play. Several UK firms are world-class aerospace/defence companies, and may be appropriate partners for Canadian exporters; they include British Aerospace (civilian and defence aerospace, ordnance), GEC-Marconi (Europe's second-largest defence electronics contractor, perhaps soon to be merged with BAe), Vickers Defence Systems (armoured vehicles), GKN Westland Helicopters, Rolls-Royce (aero-engines), Pilkington Optronics (electro-optics), Shorts (missiles), Racal (electronics), Vosper Thorneycroft (patrol boats and strike craft), Lucas (aerospace systems), Dowty (landing gear, propellers), Smiths (flight management and avionics systems), and Pilatus Britten-Norman (small aircraft).

More than 400 Canadian companies or subsidiaries have investments in Britain including Alcan, Nortel, Bombardier (Short Brothers), Magna (Multimatics), Newbridge, CDC, Allied Signal, Indal, and Litton. In 1994, for the first time ever, the stock of Canadian investment in the UK exceeded the stock of British investment in Canada. The total value of two-way investment today exceeds $30 billion, with Canadians investing $16.7 billion in Britain, against British investments of $14.2 billion in Canada. Although most of this investment is in the civilian sector, some of it will necessarily also fall into the realm of defence industrial cooperation, such are the trends of a globalizing defence industry.

In addition to the NATO operations mentioned above, Canada and the UK work together in some purely bilateral operations, such as the joint maritime course. Starting in 1999, the UK's new amphibious support ship, *HMS Ocean*, has been conducting some of her workups off Newfoundland, alongside Canadian ships. As the UK moves more toward a joint-force operating mentality, we can expect to see further interaction along these lines.

Canada has integrated its forces at the grass-roots levels. In truth, we have had to "disintegrate" in certain areas. Interestingly, the UK Strategic Defence Review emphasizes joint and rapid-reaction capabilities. Our own experiences in this regard are both different and of longer duration; thus there is need and scope for liaison and mutual learning. This should provide the opportunity to progress via higher-level staff talks (e.g., the Navy-to-Navy talks held every 18 months). In fact, we found during the NATO long-term study that the UK and Canada supported each other against the rest of the pack in several cases. Instances included giving priority to operational efficiency, so as to save money and increase capability, as compared with costs associated with superfluous NATO headquarters.

A final area of bilateral cooperation has been peacekeeping, peacemaking, and peace-support operations. We have established (jointly funded by DFAIT and DND) a centre of excellence privately run to train peacekeepers in the New Peacekeeping Partnership, stressing interaction and coordination between military and civilian, governmental and non-governmental, efforts. Various levels of courses are offered at the Lester B. Pearson International Peacekeeping Training Centre in Cornwallis, Nova Scotia. We are always seeking more UK participation in these very critical courses in operations other than war.

IV

I offer some closing comments on the transatlantic link. Canada is the largest trading partner of our great American neighbour. We do more business with the US than all of Europe does, and the same applies, obviously, in respect of Japan. Yet there is a frequent tendency for observers, on both sides of the Atlantic, to overlook Canada when the discussion turns to security and defence matters, and in particular to the mooted European Security and Defence Identity (ESDI). This is not intentional neglect, and indeed stems in part from Canada's own reluctance to enhance its visibility. In the spirit of the Denver agreement, we would like our British friends and allies to strive to build the emerging transatlantic partnership — in both its economic and security dimensions — on an inclusive not exclusive basis. Canada may only have slightly more than 10 percent of America's population (30 million compared with 260 million), but we are tied with the US through an umbilical defence cord.

I would like to envision a future for transatlantic and bilateral (Canada-UK) defence cooperation in which there is:

• an enhancement of Canada's visibility, particularly that of our high-tech Navy, within NATO;

• an increased presence of Canadian high-tech companies in the UK market, so as to achieve operational and economic efficiencies;

• a NATO Flying Training program in Canada with a strong RAF presence;

• a pattern of joint operations on a regular basis with increased bilateral effort;

• a continuation of major equipment purchases by Canada from the UK, and a stimulation of reciprocal arrangements (industrial benefits notwithstanding);

• greater exchange of personnel between the services of the two countries;

• a continuation of international operations, side-by-side in NATO through its Standing Naval Forces (Channel, Mediterranean, and Atlantic); and

• an increase in the frequency of military and civilian interchanges and colloquia (such as the 1998 Canada-UK Colloquium in Halifax) focused upon the military dimension of the bilateral relationship.

It bears remembering that the very core of our bilateral relationship has, historically, been a military one. From it have developed and flourished the relationship's diverse dimensions, whether these be in the areas of trade, investment, or culture.

I would close with some quotations from a book I co-authored with Sharon Hobson, entitled *The Persian Excursion*. These passages epitomize the Canadian military perspective — a perspective that permeates all that a middle power such as Canada does in the world:

> It's the Canadian navy ... Take a whole hodge podge of stuff and put it together and make it work. We've taken a Dutch fire control system and married it with an Italian gun in the Tribal class destroyers and it works, and everybody looks at this and asks "How on earth did you do that?"

Canadians do it, Canadians make it work. The US works on brute strength and the latest technology, and if it's simple even better. Some of the Europeans work on very intricate and complex systems. The British produce good solid equipment — if it's built to withstand a direct hit it's British. And Canadians have looked at all of this and said, "Yeah, there's a time to be able to use each of those philosophies — let's put them together." And it's the putting them together that's the challenge. That's where we excel.

Over the years we have consciously sought to have our equipment compatible with that of the United States. This proved invaluable given that communications, cryptographic, and weapons systems need a common basis for both operations and maintenance. When we were getting ready for the Gulf we added some British equipment knowing that they would be major players in the crisis. Some countries with only national type communications equipment were hamstrung during the war given that they could not receive the complete range of information available.

We are not British, we are not American, we are not French. We are part of each and yet unique in ourselves. We are a Canadian cultural mosaic and proud of it. Long may we have lots in common.

Acknowledgements

The world of security and defence is being transformed at the dawn of a new century by sweeping changes, including the end of the Cold War, new strategic doctrines, the revolution in information technologies, the impact of globalization on the defence industrial base, and constraints on government spending. In this book, experts from Canada and the United Kingdom analyze these changes and explore the challenges they create.

Security, Strategy and the Global Economics of Defence Production represents a contribution to policy debates from the Canada-United Kingdom Colloquia. Each year, the Colloquia bring together parliamentarians, policymakers, academics, representatives from the private sector, members of the media and other social commentators from both countries to discuss important policy issues. Inaugurated in 1984, the Colloquia constitute an integral part of the relationship between the two countries, confirming the contemporary relevance of a link deeply embedded in history. The role of the Colloquia was highlighted by Prime Ministers Blair and Chrétien in a joint declaration issued during the Denver summit of the G7 countries in 1997, and again in 1998 when Prime Minister Chrétien paid an official visit to London.

The Colloquia are sustained by a unique four-way partnership. They are supported by the Department of Foreign Affairs and International Trade in Canada and the Foreign and Commonwealth Office in the UK. They are organized by the School of Policy Studies of Queen's University on the Canadian side, and the British Committee of the Canada-United Kingdom Colloquia in the UK.

This book flows from a colloquium held in November 1998 in the historic city of Halifax, Nova Scotia, a city steeped in military life. We would like to thank David Haglund of Queen's University and Neil MacFarlane of Oxford University for serving as editors of the book, and the contributors from both sides of the Atlantic whose thoughts are captured between its covers.

Security, Strategy and the Global Economics of Defence Production is the second title in a new series published for the Colloquia by McGill-Queen's University

Press. We would like to thank the Publications Unit of the School of Policy Studies and McGill-Queen's University Press. The happy partnership between these two organizations has made the series a reality, and we extend our appreciation to Mark Howes, Philip Cercone and their respective teams for their support.

Geoffrey Bacon   *Keith G. Banting*
Chairman, British Committee   *Director*
Canada-United Kingdom Colloquia   *School of Policy Studies*

1

Introduction

David G. Haglund and S. Neil MacFarlane

As the recent war against Serbia has demonstrated, the technology of modern warfare is in constant evolution, with implications that will be debated for years to come. Those implications span a wide range of public policy areas, from the broad dimensions of alliance strategy to the specific confines of defence investment, production, and trade. For the past several years, technological innovation in the arms industry of the world's leading states has been proceeding apace with the phenomenon of "globalization" in the civilian sector. Although the combined impact of the postulated "revolution in military affairs" and the globalization of industry has been felt in all Western states, it has been a particular concern in two NATO countries, Canada and the United Kingdom, located as each is on the margins of a continental market in defence goods within which has been or may be established a set of privileged linkages and interests.

It is true that the continentalization of defence industry developed much more quickly and intensively in North America than in Europe; indeed, in the latter continent it has remained, until very recently, very much a will-o'-the-wisp. But change looks to be occurring in Europe, where defence industries are finally embarked on a necessary journey on the road to consolidation, in a long-overdue bid to eliminate excess capacity and restore (or create) competitiveness vis-à-vis an American defence industry that began the painful process of adapting to new market realities nearly a decade ago. It is not just Europe that appears, however tardily, to be changing; ironically, as states in Western Europe evince a desire for further defence industrial integration, it can sometimes look as if in North America a period of "disintegration" has begun, even if not by design.

The result is that of NATO's 19 members, it is the two continental "outriders," Canada and the United Kingdom, that face the most intriguing challenges of adjustment in coming years. Canada must seek to preserve the North American defence industrial base (NADIBO) against further erosion, while at the same time position itself as skillfully as it can in respect of the European market. Canada's interests will be best served if the West's emerging defence industrial base takes shape along transatlantic lines, rather than developing as two distinct "pillars" within NATO's overarching structure. There may be little Canada can actually *choose* to do that will make a significant difference to its future defence industrial development; nevertheless, it will be profoundly affected, as it has been for some time, by the choices of others.

Among those others, the United Kingdom ranks second in importance only to the United States. What Britain decides will have major bearing on whether Canadian industry will be able to realize the defence industrial base it prefers to have instead of the one it must have. For their part, the British will need to decide whether they will, as the Blair government has indicated they would, blend their defence capability more completely into a European Security and Defence Identity (ESDI), with all that this will imply for their defence industries. It will be Britain, more than any other European state, that will have the ability to steer the construction of the Western alliance's defence industrial base along those transatlantic lines preferred by Canada.

But the future shape of the West's defence industrial base is only one of the questions the authors of this volume explore. Indeed, how one configures a defence industrial base will have much to do with the apprehended future security challenges facing both Canada and the UK, either singly or, more likely, as part of a broader coalition of states. And how states will acquire what they think they need will be mightily conditioned by the evolution of military technology, just as it will be by the willingness and ability of Western publics to spend on defence, as well as to understand and accept a certain degree of contradiction between what is politically desirable (as in the matter of export controls) and what is politically feasible.

This volume's examination of these related policy issues comprises three substantive parts, and a conclusion. In Part One, our contributors provide the background for understanding what it is the two countries have done together in the past, and for comprehending the security challenges they may be confronting in the future. Part Two is given over to assessing the relative merits of regional defence industrial blocs as opposed to transatlantic arrangements. In Part Three our authors concentrate upon policy and budgetary considerations of greatest likely impact upon Canadian and British defence industrial debates, including such issues as procurement reform, subsidization, industrial and regional benefits, and export controls.

William Hopkinson's chapter serves as a useful reminder that while bilateral defence cooperation will never approximate the level of integration achieved at the start of this century (when, after all, Canada was very much dependent on Britain's lead in foreign and security policy), there remains a great deal of commonality in the manner in which the two countries pursue defence. As recent operations in the Balkans reveal (both in Bosnia and Serbia), Canada and Britain "can and do operate together now as well as in the past, even though the causes and scales are very different." Especially is this the case with ground forces. Still, there are notable differences in the way the two countries approach certain aspects of defence and security policy, and Hopkinson notes in particular a Canadian lack of "hard-headedness" at times (*viz.*, the anti-personnel land-mines treaty), and a Canadian indifference to paying as much for defence as may be required.

Whatever else the future holds in store, says Hopkinson, there will continue to be a need for Canada, Britain, and other states to intervene in crises somewhere in the world. It is upon the topic of future crises and responses that Fen Hampson's chapter is concentrated. A hallmark of the post-Cold War world has been the rise of intrastate conflict at the same time as the risk of major war has radically diminished (though the author cautions against the view that the risk of interstate war is now so low as to be negligible). A second characteristic involves technology: more and more actors — not all of them states — are endowed with the ability to project violence over great distances, and Hampson notes the current tendency of many analysts to speak of "megaterrorism." In response to the challenges posed by revisionist states and non-state entities, crisis management will increasingly take the form of coalitions of the willing and the able. Almost certainly, Britain and Canada will form part of such coalitions, especially as these are constituted from a core of allied states. More so than in the recent past, such coalitions will have to grapple with important questions associated with interoperability and the incorporation of new military technology.

In short, the coming years will feature a great deal of discussion about the impact of the "revolution in military affairs" (RMA). Our next two chapters, respectively by Neil MacFarlane and Thierry Gongora, address that impact. MacFarlane reminds us that current technological developments are intricately linked with societal attitudes toward warfare, especially in the West, where states are increasingly unwilling to absorb major costs in pursuit of policy aims, and seek to fight a war on as bloodless (for us) a basis as possible. Despite some obvious advantages of the RMA, detected both in the Gulf War and in the war against Serbia, it must be asked whether the future of intervention really will be characterized by conflicts in which Western technological assets can be advantageously utilized; for if the future of armed struggle is to resemble the recent past in Rwanda, then it may be that the "most significant weapons innovation in the 1990s was not the movement of war into space, but the return of the machete."

The RMA is often invoked, but rarely analyzed in the context of previous radical changes in the manner in which military power was amassed and projected. Thierry Gongora insists on a distinction between the RMA and a much more profound transformation called the "military revolution," of which there have only been a handful in the previous three centuries. While discussions of the RMA tend to focus upon the impact of information technology on "military productivity," military revolutions also involve linked transformations in size and composition of military forces, the financing of defence, and the shape of the defence industrial base. Do changes in the latter sphere portend the onset of a military revolution? Gongora suggests, tentatively, that they do not. Nor is there anything radically different about the financing of defence. "In short," he concludes, "it is still premature to speak of a military revolution, but the evolution of these fundamental indicators ... could lead to a reassessment."

One of those "fundamental indicators," the shape of the defence industrial base, frames the analysis of the three chapters of Part Two. Is the West's defence industrial base truly being "globalized," asks the author of the first of these chapters, Sir Geoffrey Pattie? While globalization is a label typically applied to transformations in a variety of economic domains (e.g., finance, civilian manufacturing) does it really fit when talk turns to the defence industries? The author suggests that "regionalization" might better capture the essence of change in the defence industrial sector, and he notes apropos the recent enthusiasm for an ESDI, that the "current debate in Europe is most surely about the Europeanization, *not* the globalization, of defence." Still, he concludes by observing, with the experience of his own company (GEC) in mind, that it may be impossible (and certainly would be undesirable) for the current defence industrial restructuring to stop at the European level; transatlantic integration is likely to become the next step in the process. In that event, it would be appropriate to claim that globalization was, after all, occurring.

Trevor Taylor's chapter continues with this theme. To Taylor, the future of the West's defence industrial base will speak to more than the mooted globalization of the defence industry; it will signal the prospects of the future health of the Atlantic alliance itself. "It must be asked," he writes, "whether the alliance could flourish if the transatlantic defence industrial scene was to be completely dominated by competitive, adversarial relationships, or if European defence businesses were overtly subservient to those of the US." Can mutually beneficial collaboration take place on a transatlantic basis? The question is not rhetorical, for the record of intra-European collaboration is, at best, mixed; as for that of transatlantic collaboration, Taylor quotes an American aerospace executive (Norman Augustine) to the effect that it has been "unblemished by success." Interestingly,

Europe today is moving away from the old model of inter*state* collaboration in favour of the creation of genuinely multinational defence companies. Will the US government, and American companies, be able to react in a constructive manner to this transformation? Taylor is doubtful: "sadly, there are signs that overall, the US will be reluctant to encourage the emergence of potentially rival defence firms in Europe."

What the US might be willing to encourage is the formation of a transatlantic defence industrial base in which American firms and European (especially British) firms combine in a variety of manners, from joint ventures on specific projects to outright mergers; in such a scenario, which to be realized would require an unprecedented willingness on the part of the US to be reliant upon overseas suppliers of defence equipment, the risk of "fortress" building on either side of the Atlantic could be kept at bay by transatlantic investment and other private-sector initiatives. *Mutatis mutandis*, a transatlantic defence industrial base might be erected on a "Canadianized" model. This, at least, is the prospect raised in the chapter by David Haglund: to what extent can the debate over transatlantic defence integration be informed by the analysis of North American defence integration? Although there are significant differences — including geostrategic ones — between the Canadian and Western European experience, perhaps the differences have been exaggerated. It is sometimes said in Europe that retaining an autonomous defence industrial capacity is indispensable for national survival. Haglund concludes, however, that "[u]nless one can foresee a time when Europe and the United States become strategic rivals, ... it becomes more and more difficult to make the case that Europe's *political* future — or at least its 'survival' — depends in any meaningful way upon its having a defence industrial base that is relatively autonomous from the North American one."

Part Three is concerned with policy options and policy dilemmas. Paul Manson begins the analysis by asking "who defends the defence industry" in Canada? In an era characterized by the relative retreat of the state from a variety of policy areas, what levers are left to be pulled by those intent on fashioning a defence industrial policy? The ending of the Cold War has made defence policy seem less of a public priority, and not just in Canada. As a result, defence spending and spending for capital equipment have each declined substantially, so that today Ottawa spends $9 billion on defence, with only 16 percent of that amount available for investment in capital procurement. There are some changes that can be made at the margin by government — in particular the streamlining of a capital-equipment procurement process deemed by the author to be "ludicrously cumbersome" — but Manson looks instead to industry to solve the problems of the defence industrial base. This latter, he concludes, "has been internationalized, if not globalized, within the community of democratic countries, as part of the free market economy. In other words, the defence of the defence industry is ultimately the responsibility of companies, not of governments."

James Fergusson's chapter is similarly concerned with the Canadian defence budget, and the obstacles to more effective output for dollars invested in defence. The obstacles are to be found less at the level of strategy — for here Fergusson does find a degree of policy coherence enunciated in the 1994 *Defence White Paper*'s "expressed strategic preference," namely that Canada contribute to international peace and stability — and more at the level of willingness to spend to honour strategic commitments. A "commitment-capability" gap is nothing new in Canadian defence; if anything, it represents the norm, and for years the Canadian Forces (CF) have become more specialized as one means of reducing the gap. But specialization alone has its (fast-approaching) limits, meaning that reforms are needed in other areas of defence — procurement, above all. Here Fergusson echoes the observations of Manson, and cites the numerous political encumbrances of a process that appears not to be geared to obtaining the most rational relationship between "inputs" and outcomes. But he also parts company from Manson, for to Fergusson it can often be the *political* lobbying efforts of defence industry that contribute to the inefficiencies of the procurement process, as demonstrated by the long saga to find a replacement helicopter for Canada's aged Sea King. The need to procure more creatively will be more compelling in future, given that defence capital investments are hardly expected to increase. To the ongoing challenge, Fergusson concludes, has been added the problem of assuring interoperability with close allies; "for Canada does not fight alone, and unless the CF are interoperable, they may not be able to fight at all."

A recent policy dilemma facing the UK has been the question of arms exports. Philip Gummett takes the reader through an analysis of the issue from the perspective of a country (Britain) that ranks second only to the US as an arms exporter yet has recently pledged to adopt a more "ethical" stance on the selling of weaponry. Can the circle be squared of trying to retain and enhance the vitality of the country's defence industrial base while not, at the same time, contributing to the exacerbation of regional and global security problems through an imprudent promotion of arms sales? To understand the challenge it is important to grasp why Britain (or any other country) deems arms exports to be so important. Gummett identifies three reasons for states to export arms: security dictates, political interests, and economic returns. Of the three, the latter seems to be most persuasive today, even though it is far from obvious what those economic returns really are for society, given alternative uses to which state revenues could be put. Since Labour came to power in May 1997, there has been some good basis to believe that substantive tightening of British (and European Union) export codes is in the offing. Gummett argues that, on balance, such a tightening makes sense, even though an economic price may have to be paid for such instances of "good international citizenship." On his reading of the evidence, that price would be worth paying.

Nor is it simply Britain under Labour that has been revisiting its export policy. Canada, too, as Claire Turenne Sjolander argues, has had to wrestle with the same trade-off as that identified by Gummett, between the economic advantages accruing from the export of defence equipment and the security disadvantages stemming from exports that get into the wrong hands. Both countries seek, to the extent possible, to concentrate their foreign sales in the market of like-minded Western states, preferably allies. But this is not always possible. Nor is it always possible, given the "dual-use" nature of many high technology goods, ostensibly "civilian" but able to be put to military purposes, to control the imprudent transfer of equipment to undesirable consumers. Exports may not even, in future, be such a concern from the ethical standpoint, given the globalization trend in the West's (and the world's) defence industrial base, particularly if the increase in collaborative ventures, especially as between private industries, results, as it logically must, in the diffusion of defence-related technology. As Turenne Sjolander explains, globalization means that the "control of exports is in some respects impossible, and potentially moot.... Anything short of a universal export control regime will not defend national, or global, security interests."

The concluding chapter, by Denis Stairs, draws upon the other chapters in this volume as well as the discussion that took place at the Colloquium, and offers a synthesis of the major themes debated during the Halifax meeting, and reproduced in these pages. Stairs illustrates the manner in which both Canada and the United Kingdom approach defence problems, sometimes in a similar fashion, but at other times in a way that betrays an acute difference in historical memory and current standing as between a Western hemisphere "middle power" and a former European great power. Overall, he notes, the discussion that took place in Halifax was "extraordinarily rich, engagingly candid, and impressively detailed. There can be no doubt that 'old country' folk and 'new country' folk still know how to talk to one another." Despite the conviction of some observers who detect in various objective indicators a slackening of bilateral ties, it is clear that on the topic of their defence interests and industries, there remains considerable common ground linking Canada with the United Kingdom, and that "in the encounters of *cognoscenti*, the conversations are still infused with a sense of the familiar, and with the recognition that both parties are somehow rooted in the same place."

Part One

HISTORICAL AND STRATEGIC CONTEXT

2

Canada-United Kingdom Defence Cooperation

William Hopkinson

INTRODUCTION

The title of this chapter presents a very tall order for such a short recounting. Even an historical survey would be a major undertaking. If one tries to look into the future the questions become very complex. There are a large number of inter-locking issues, ranging from sensitive historical questions, to some real difficul-ties in foreseeing future industrial organization and relationships between the United States and Europe. I shall try to look both forwards and backwards, to reflect on some important historical associations, though not seek to trace matters back before the later part of the nineteenth century, and to think about the lessons of more recent history for the future.

THE HISTORICAL LEGACY

Until about 1885 the defence of the British Columbia coast was a much discussed imperial strategic problem; thereafter Canada's ability to contribute to imperial defence came to the fore. It was seen as having a loyal militia with large numbers of fishermen suitable for use as a naval reserve. What was more, the recruit from Canada would be an outdoor type, not a pale-faced artisan! The museum in Hali-fax records the first less-than-successful attempt to endow Canada with its own naval asset; early in the twentieth century a more successful effort led to the found-ing of the Royal Canadian Navy. The development of that, and the enjoyment and exercise of a common naval heritage, have been important for both Canada and the UK in this century, but it was the participation of Canada's land forces in

World War I that was particularly significant from the point of view of nation-building.

By the spring of 1917, four Canadian divisions were in the field, with a fifth division in England. The entire corps fought together for the first time in April 1917, when it distinguished itself at Vimy Ridge. Many of us will have stood on that ridge and visited the great Canadian Memorial. Less well known is the part played by the Canadian Corps' operations in the last few months of that war. This was a time when the British Army (including this force) was winning victories and advancing at speeds similar to those achieved in the advances of World War II. The Canadian Corps had a particular role in this inasmuch as it was stronger than comparable British formations, and its operations were conducted with great skill and imagination. From the "Black Day of the German Army" on 8 August 1918 the British forces, spearheaded to a large extent by the Canadian Corps, advanced over 100 km. Perhaps never before or since have Canadian troops played such a decisive role, and in saying that I have not forgotten D-Day, or Bomber Command.

The Canadian Corps earned an enviable record as a fighting force and represented the first authentic expression of Canada in the world, although the cost to Canada was high. Out of approximately 625,000 who served, about 60,000 were killed in action or died in active service, and another 173,000 were wounded. Other aspects of the war effort were equally impressive. Canadian foodstuffs and raw materials were of first importance in maintaining the Allies, as were the millions of shells turned out by Canadian factories.

In World War II, Canada's effort was even more extensive. By its end, more than 1,000,000 Canadians had served in the three services. Casualties were lower than in the previous war, with approximately 42,000 killed or having died in service, and 54,400 wounded. The domestic war effort was no less significant. Canada hosted, and paid much of the cost of, the British Commonwealth Air Training Plan, which trained more than 100,000 Commonwealth airmen. Canadian factories turned out everything from rifles to Lancaster heavy bombers, and Canadian scientists, technicians, and engineers worked on advanced weapons technology, including the atomic bomb (for which Canada supplied the uranium ore). Canadian foods, direct cash contributions to Britain, and munitions for the Allies, including the Soviet Union, contributed to the overall war effort. The overall impact on Canadian society was even more profound.

I make two observations from this brief history. The first is that "Canadian" and "British" need not be antithetical terms; one has embraced the other. The First World War marked a turning point in Canadian development and the Statute of Westminster later changed forever the relationship with the Dominions. Nevertheless, even in World War II the degree of integration of British and Canadian forces was considerable, from individuals and individual crews in the Royal Air Force, to the Normandy landings. We shall not see such integration again, at any rate on anything approaching that scale. Nevertheless — and this is my second observation — in terms of doctrine, methodology, and objectives, our land forces still have much more in common than either has with American forces. Militaries in both countries are under a different sort of political control from that exercised from Washington. The interchange of individuals, and the access to staff colleges, has provided a sound basis for that to continue.

THE ENDURING PATTERN OF COOPERATION

In considering both defence industrial and military issues, certainly for the present and the future if not for the past, my main point revolves around our relations with, but crucial differences from, the United States. Militaries in both our countries are under a different sort of political control from that in the US. There is not the pernicious doctrine of "overwhelming force." There is a different respect for the role of international law and the United Nations (UN). Our militaries can and will collaborate on a wide range of issues dealing with the security problems of the coming century that, for the most part, will involve failed states, rather than world-war type aggression. A common basis of training doctrine and procedures, coming partly from NATO but also in large measure from a common non-NATO heritage, will stand that collaboration in good stead.

If we consider security rather than military cooperation, there is, of course, a long-standing intelligence relationship between our two countries. It would be inappropriate to dwell on that here at length, but it is important that, as new threats emerge, we all develop and maintain the necessary intelligence gathering and processing facilities. Again, though lacking US technology, we can both put in a credible performance from what our troops can gather on the ground. A certain similarity of doctrine, patrolling on foot rather than in groups of four armoured vehicles, helps. For all sorts of reasons it is most important that we keep up our collaboration at the higher levels too.

Partway between military and industrial collaboration there has been a long history of scientific collaboration. I recently noted with interest that some of the very early work on nuclear matters was done before World War I, at McGill University. (The fact that Rutherford was a New Zealander, though not directly relevant, is another demonstration of Empire.) The history of Canadian defence research can be traced back to World War I, when Canadian scientists worked on the danger from submarines and sea-mines in the Atlantic. Twenty years later, during World War II, Canada's effort was more substantial. By the end of the war, Canada had a strong competence in defence research and development and to this day the Research and Development (R&D) Branch contributes to the collective defence research efforts of Canada's allies.

I should just like to mention one aspect of collaborative effort that still, I believe, continues: work on defence against chemical weapons (CW). That is something helpful not only in developing the subject but also in raising consciousness of the issues. On weapons of mass destruction (WMD) there is a twofold problem: some players, knowing the potential of biological or chemical weapons, get matters quite out of perspective and distort upwards the priority to be given to such matters. Others, in ignorance, do not realize the potential dangers from a lack of firm control. I believe that both Canada and the United Kingdom are admirably balanced on these issues.

I am not competent to trace the full history of defence industrial collaboration between the United Kingdom and Canada. I shall not even try. What I should like to do is draw certain parallels in our situations, again, as in purely military matters, looking particularly at relations with the US. As a preliminary, however, I should like to register two points. First, since the 1960s the UK and Canada have seen their relative mutual dependence decline. That is not to undervalue the role that particular companies play in each other's economy. The fact is, however, that the US is likely to figure much more than either with the other.

The second and more important point is the changing nature of defence industry. No medium-sized nation is now able to build a complete advanced system. Partnership is the word, and that means having a network of relationships with different partners for different projects. Moreover, the key and most difficult aspect of defence work is likely to be the integration of complex systems, not the production of individual components. That, in turn, is linked to the fact that defence is generally no longer at the cutting edge of individual developments. Civilian technologies are often in the lead, and the military procurement task is in large part ensuring that the latest benefits and products of the civilian sector are successfully incorporated.

DEFENCE INDUSTRIAL BASE ISSUES

Both our countries are advanced Western nations with skilled workforces and developed industries. In each case, however, we are in some sense overshadowed, or at least profoundly affected, by the US, which has a much larger economy, highly competitive pay rates, and a bigger research and scientific base. In each case we obtain much benefit, technical and economic, from close collaboration with the US. In each case, however, there is a concern to avoid being swamped, overwhelmed, or simply eaten by that larger partner.

The US has recently rationalized its defence industries to make itself an even more formidable player. For many reasons, Europe too must sort out its defence industries, not to create a fortress Europe, or to foster a "buy-European" policy. The UK could not deny itself the ability to pursue value for money by buying American in appropriate cases. Even more cogently, UK industry is a major supplier to the US defence industry and many projects now require a collaborative or consortial approach. The UK's interest lies in a more open transatlantic market, in which it can compete on relatively equal terms. It must be able to put together partnerships with US players and with others too.

Canada has its own privileged arrangements with the US, at least in principle. Under the Canada-US Defence Production Sharing Arrangement (DPSA), Canadian companies are generally allowed to compete for prime and subcontracts on the same basis as American companies. The DPSA provides a broad access, particularly in the components and combat systems of ships, aircraft, and vehicles. The Defence Development Sharing Arrangement (DDSA) is an adjunct of the DPSA for developing defence products and technology. In theory, Canadian companies generally compete for US defence acquisition on the same terms as American companies with the *Buy American Act* waived. However, in practice, there are restrictions, the most significant include US national security and Buy American applications in the annual *Authorization and Appropriations Acts.*

For the UK, effective partnership requires rationalization of the European defence industries, and there is a very long way to go on that. The UK has done a considerable amount; Germany recognizes the need; France may or may not. The sorting out of European industry need not preclude close UK-Canadian cooperation, nor indeed close Canadian collaboration with other European players. That will, however, require the creation of Canadian companies with sufficient financial and technical strength to be good partners. It also may raise questions about the role of US companies as shareholders or players on the Canadian scene. It is difficult to be specific on precisely what Canada should be seeking, but aiming at the high value-added rather than the heavy-metal end is clearly the right course. There will be opportunities for UK-Canadian collaboration, and some important examples could be cited from current arrangements. However, major defence industry rationalization is not likely to be a principal axis of the two countries working together.

BROADER POLICY CONCERNS

My own interests and concerns are not with industrial matters but with policy: why we have defence forces, what we use them for, and how they are used. In all these areas, I am certain that Canada and the UK have much to say to each other.

They have a common historical heritage. That is not simply a matter of sentiment, though sentiment should not be neglected; what people feel is important, and what a nation believes about itself, for good or ill, does affect what happens in the arena of world politics.

We have a common belief in the importance of international law; we are neither of us likely to believe that simple unilateral assertion of force is a sufficient basis for international action. Our militaries think and act in much the same way. Despite some unfortunate recent incidents, both countries have an honourable record of engaging in various messy situations. We can and do operate together now as well as in the past, even though the causes and scales are very different. Intervention is likely to be *the* key issue of international relations over the next 20 years and the UK and Canada are well placed to develop appropriate international law on that, appropriate military doctrine on how it should be done, and, probably, to have useful lessons to teach each other on motivating military personnel to engage effectively in nasty disputes, far from home, where neither the ashes of their fathers nor the temples of their gods are involved.

Before leaving the question of international law I should wish to make one short point on moral or ethical issues. Humanitarian law is important, and is an area where both the UK and Canada have good records. It is necessary to be clear, however, that kind sentiments are not sufficient. A degree of hard-headedness is also necessary. There have been examples in recent years where true alleviation of suffering has perhaps been hindered rather than helped by various initiatives. My personal view is that the anti-personnel land-mines treaty was a mistake in substance, and certainly in how it was achieved. The mischief that land mines have done has been enormous; the feelings of revulsion understandable. Whether the right target was selected and the right action taken on this issue is much more debatable. This is not the place to argue that in detail; the short point is that a desire to do good is not sufficient, and there has sometimes been in the Canadian body politic a lack of appreciation of that. However, the development of humanitarian law is an area in which countries serious about both defence and international norms may take part. There is much to be done in elaborating international rules on intervention and on the conduct of military operations. UK and Canada, by history and politics, are well placed to work together on that.

Intervention requires, of course, investment of resources as well as the display of will. After a period of unfortunate underinvestment in its armed forces, Canada has recently undertaken procurement more in line with its status and perceived role in the world. That said, it is legitimate to ask whether it has yet faced questions of sustainability and regeneration, of lift, and of the need to engage with allies to tackle the most difficult and distant questions. If Canada is to be serious as a supporter of international order it will have to invest in hardware and training for the heavier end of the spectrum of military activity. Intervention in the next century will not be simple peacekeeping with lightly armed forces. There will have to be a manifest capability to fight. To be taken seriously a country has to demonstrate that it is serious.

Meanwhile the US brings much to the party that at present neither Canada nor any European state can match. The question is about the terms on which the US will engage, and those on which we can and should support the US where general Western interests are involved. NATO is one forum for influencing the US and it is unfortunate that in recent years Canada's influence and impact there have been diminished, as a result of cutbacks. There are other fora that will increase in importance. We have seen the Contact Group for former Yugoslavia; there is the G7/8. There remains the UN, of great importance though uncertain development. The UK is a player, and an active one in most such fora; I believe that it will remain so. Directoires of various sorts, even though the term arouses understandable resistance, will be a feature of the conduct of diplomacy in the future. Where Canada cannot be a direct member, it may be that close collaboration with the UK should be a part of its armoury. An issue of particular interest, partly for historical reasons, but partly also by virtue of the complex relationships with the US, will be the EU-US dialogue. In many ways Canada is like a European state; it too has a vital relationship with the US, but does not wish to be swamped. There are good arguments for much closer EU-Canada dialogue as part of the wider transatlantic relationship.

CONCLUSION

To conclude then, Canada and the UK have an almost unparalleled history of effective military cooperation. We feel at ease with each other. Our militaries work well and share the same ethical and doctrinal approaches. They are efficient. We each have a special relationship with the US, but that should not be the whole of our defence relationships. The US is different in size, in politics, and in its approach to international relations. Without discarding what we have to gain from relations with the US, Canada and the UK can and should work together at every level from the individual officer on secondment, through doctrinal development, to actual military collaboration on the ground, and up to cooperation in the UN to develop better international law on intervention. We shall both gain from that, and so will the international community.

3

The Changing Nature of International Conflict: Challenges and Responses

Fen Osler Hampson

INTRODUCTION

The purpose of this chapter is to discuss the changing nature of international conflict, with a view to outlining some of the main security challenges that policymakers on both sides of the Atlantic confront as the century ends. I start by addressing the changing nature of violent conflict in the international system. After this, I briefly outline some important impacts of technology on the new security agenda, including the problems of "rogue states" and terrorist groups. I then turn to contemporary trends in defence spending and research, following which I sketch the different institutional tools of conflict management that have evolved to address these new security challenges. Lastly, I delimit some of the core operational and technical challenges policymakers face if these new institutional arrangements are to work effectively.

CHANGING NATURE OF INTERNATIONAL CONFLICT

Identifying the main patterns and causes of armed conflict in the international system is a risky exercise. Conventional wisdom has proved to be more often wrong than right. Take the case of the mooted "new world order." As the Cold War was ending in the wake of the collapse of the Berlin Wall, presidents, prime ministers, and the occasional foolhardy pundit spoke about such a global order. This was to be based upon an absence of systemic conflict between the great powers of the international system, and in particular upon a new spirit of cooperation between the two superpowers. In a major address before the General Assembly of the United Nations in December 1988, Soviet leader Mikhail Gorbachev laid out his vision for a reinvigorated United Nations (UN) and a Security Council in which the great powers would work together to resolve their differences and negotiate an end to the violent "proxy wars" that had been the hallmark of much conflict in the Third World (Hampson 1989).

To be sure, that spirit of cooperation helped to defuse tensions and bring about peace in Cambodia, Southern Africa, Central America, and Afghanistan. But as was quickly discovered when new conflicts sprouted in Africa, Asia, and elsewhere, the "proxy" elements of conflict, namely the US-Soviet rivalry, had only been part of the equation in many Third World regional conflicts. The collapse of the Soviet Union itself, and the rise of new states along Russia's borders, also created new tensions and rivalries, many of which were rooted in violent ethnic clashes between different minority groups.

Realizing that a new world order was not in the offing, analysts began to speak instead about a "post-Cold War world." The chief difference between the Cold War and post-Cold War era, many believed, was the rise of intrastate conflict and the decline of systemic or system-wide conflict (Axworthy 1997). As noted in the SIPRI yearbook, in 1997 there were 25 major armed conflicts in 24 locations throughout the world. This compared to 27 armed conflicts in 24 locations in 1996 — a number that was still appreciably lower than those for 1989, the year many say the Cold War ended.

All but one of the conflicts in 1997 were internal, that is to say, the conflict was about the control of government or territory within the state. The sole case of interstate conflict in 1997 was the conflict between India and Pakistan over Kashmir. All of the new conflicts in 1997 were on the African continent. They included the conflict in Burundi between the Tutsi-dominated government and the Hutu-based opposition, the short civil war in Congo, the conflict in Zaire which had actually began a year earlier, and the protracted conflict in Senegal over the territory of Casamance (Rotfeld 1998; Sollenberg and Wallensteen 1998).

Although the existence of intrastate conflict is one of the defining features of the post-Cold War period, it would be a mistake to discount the continued potential for interstate conflict in international relations (Crocker and Hampson 1996). This is despite the new conventional wisdom in some foreign policy circles that intrastate conflict — what is sometimes called the "failed state" phenomenon — is today the only kind of conflict in international relations. It is certainly the case that the probability of systemic-level conflict between the great powers of the international system is now low (assuming, of course, that China does not try explicitly and overtly to challenge current United States hegemony and that Russia remains weak), the potential for major interstate conflict continues to remain high in many regions of the globe.

In Asia, for example, the risk of war on the Indian subcontinent as a result of unresolved border disputes between India and Pakistan over Kashmir is frighteningly real; India's recent series of underground nuclear tests and Pakistan's response with tests of its own, casts a nuclear pall over this simmering conflict. In the Pacific, territorial disputes, most notably over the Spratly Islands and offshore mineral resources, including oil, divide China and its Pacific neighbours. Taiwan is also a potential flash point, as are lingering boundary disputes between some of the countries of Southeast Asia.

In Latin America, the recent conflict between Peru and Equador stands as a sharp reminder that even within the Western hemisphere interstate conflict has not altogether disappeared. Given the fragility of newly formed democratic governments, many fear that with worsening economic conditions in the region, as a result of the recent and continuing financial crisis, élites may choose to exploit boundary disputes with their neighbours to rally public support.

Within the new Europe, which extends from the Atlantic to the Urals, the treatment of national minorities in neighbouring states remains a serious problem, as it does in the Asian regions of the former Soviet Union. In these cases, the possibility of intrastate conflict escalating into interstate war is distressingly real, as the current situation in Kosovo attests. The long-standing dispute between Greece and Turkey is a stark reminder of the risks of interstate conflict even among NATO partners. Finally, in the Middle East — although much attention has been focused on the Palestinian-Israeli relationship — there are other festering disputes over water resources and borders between key states in the region that continue to threaten regional stability.

Not all of these conflicts, which, it must be noted, hardly constitute an exhaustive list, are of equal gravity or risk, but they do in a variety of ways underscore the blurred distinction between intrastate and interstate conflict.

TECHNOLOGY AND THE NEW SECURITY AGENDA

The danger of employing a crude intra- and interstate typology to characterize today's conflicts carries over into any discussion of a conflict's potential regional versus international (that is, systemic) ramifications. Longer missile and aircraft ranges, together with the growing number of states that possess the technology to build weapons of mass destruction, allow regional powers to project military capabilities on an increasingly wide, even global, scale. Accurate and more lethal weapons, better reconnaissance platforms, and a wide range of information-based military systems are revolutionizing conventional warfare, dramatically changing targeting possibilities, and raising the risks of preemptive attacks in a crisis.

New military (and non-military) technologies have the potential to empower small and medium powers, and especially "rogue states," to a far greater comparative extent than great powers. These developments are changing the character of warfare and the way various actors regard the utility of force in international relations. The proliferation of such capabilities in the context of unresolved regional tensions raises exponentially the prospects of military confrontation. The superpower rivalry may have ended with the Cold War but not the great-power aspirations of regional powers who crave the ability to project, and possibly even use, military force beyond their immediate neighbourhood. Although the forces of ethno-nationalism and religious intolerance may still be on the rise, great-power politics and rivalries over spheres of influence have not ceased. Moreover, they form a volatile mixture when combined with the centrifugal forces that threaten domestic stability in an increasing number of states (Freedman 1998; Orme 1997/ 1998).

One of the new topics of discussion among security analysts is the threat of "megaterrorism," not just terrorism. Some believe that megaterrorism, that is, efforts to take hostage or kill thousands (if not millions) of people, could also be on the rise as extremist groups of one kind or another (and not just states) gain access to the new technologies of weapons of mass destruction. Much of this debate has rather apocalyptic overtones tending to underscore that this phenomenon — or at least the potential for it — is not well understood. In fact, the number of incidents involving terrorist attacks has actually dropped during this decade. However, the number of casualties in those attacks has risen with the increase in large-scale terrorist attacks directed at inflicting massive civilian casualties (Sprinzak 1998).

There are four noteworthy trends in modern terrorism. First, terrorist violence motivated by religion is increasing. Second, opposition to foreign influences, including a military presence, is intensifying among moderate regimes in the Persian Gulf. Third, right-wing terrorism is growing in the US, Western Europe, Israel, Russia, and the former Soviet Union. Fourth, terrorist groups are increasingly comprised of "ad hoc collections of the like-minded," that is, groups of individuals who band together to carry out a single attack (Falkenrath 1998, pp. 56-59).

CONTEMPORARY TRENDS IN DEFENCE SPENDING AND RESEARCH

Although there remain a wide number of differing kinds of threats to international security, it is worth noting that worldwide military expenditure has been in decline since the late 1980s. The total amount of money devoted to military activity in 1997 was around three-quarters of a trillion US dollars or about 2.6 percent of global gross domestic product (GDP). US military expenditure has declined by about 30 percent over the past decade. In the case of Europe, military expenditures have declined by about 14 percent (Rotfeld 1998, pp. 10-11).

Global military spending on military research and development has also been in decline largely because of reductions in the US defence budget and declines in spending on R&D among the countries of the Organization for Economic Cooperation and Development (OECD). International transfers of conventional weaponry are also down. In 1997 the value of such transfers was only 62 percent of the value of such transfers in 1987.

CONFLICT MANAGEMENT RESPONSES: CHANGING INSTITUTIONAL PREFERENCES

Which, if any, identifiable trends or patterns in conflict management methods and approaches are most worthy of note? From an institutional perspective, there does appear to have been an important shift in the institutions of choice for international conflict management. At the end of the Cold War, the preferred institution of choice as conflict manager was the United Nations. It was, after all, Washington that at the January 1992 summit meeting of the heads of state of UN Security Council (UNSC) members urged the incoming secretary-general, Boutros Boutros-Ghali, to examine new ways of strengthening UN peacekeeping. His 1992 ambitious report, *An Agenda for Peace*, contained a comprehensive set of recommendations for strengthening the UN role in peacekeeping, conflict prevention, and peacebuilding. In many of the so-called multi-dimensional peacekeeping operations that took place as the Cold War was winding down, the UN was the central institutional actor. This was certainly the case in the implementation of the Angola-Namibia peace accords, the Paris peace accords in Cambodia, and other peace settlements in El Salvador, Mozambique, and Angola (Hampson 1996).

In spite of the renewed emphasis on peacekeeping, another important development in international relations was the increased willingness of the Security Council to use sanctions or the threat of force against recalcitrant members of the international system. Mandatory sanctions were used only twice by the UN during the Cold War, first against Rhodesia and then against South Africa. In the 1990s, however, they have been levied against Iraq, Yugoslavia, Libya, Haiti, UNITA in Angola, and Sierra Leone. Likewise, prior to Operation Desert Storm, the UN authorized the use of armed force in only two instances: Korea and the Congo. Including Desert Storm, since the end of the Cold War, it has authorized the use of force eight times: in Bosnia, Somalia, Haiti, Rwanda, Albania, and Zaire, as well as for Implementation Force (IFOR) operations, again in Bosnia.

With the drift of UN peacekeeping into ill-fated humanitarian and peace-enforcement interventions in Bosnia, Somalia, and Rwanda, the unwillingness of member states to rely upon UN leadership grew. Some observers concluded that the heyday of UN-directed military deployments to halt the spread of conflict had passed (Sisk and Rothchild 1997). UN-led and -managed interventions were replaced by ad hoc multilateral interventions or interventions by "coalitions of the willing." The most notable example was Operation Desert Storm — a coalition of states that was assembled by President Bush to oust Saddam Hussein's forces from Kuwait. However, in looking at the variety of ad hoc collective peacekeeping and enforcement operations of the post-Cold War period, we should note that they have not always involved the United States — for better or for worse. Some coalitions have been led by former colonial powers in Africa, as in the case of French leadership in Opération Turquoise in Rwanda. Others were initiated by middle powers as in the case of Canadian-led efforts to assemble a multinational force to intervene in Eastern Zaire in 1996 or Italy's leadership of the Multinational Protection Force that was deployed to deal with the political and humanitarian crisis in Albania in 1997 (Operation Alba).

Regional organizations were also responsible for deploying peacekeeping forces in a number of key conflicts: the Russian Commonwealth of Independent States (CIS) was responsible for peacekeeping operations in the territories of the former Soviet Union, including in the Abkhaz conflict in Georgia and the civil war in Tajikistan. In Western Africa, the Economic Community of West African States (ECOWAS) intervened in the conflict in Liberia in 1990 under a military force, ECOMOG, led by Nigeria but with participation from Ghana, Guinea, Gambia, and Sierra Leone.

These "coalitions of the willing," as the Canadian experience in Zaire attests, were not always successful. And even to the extent they were, they underscored the weakness of regional actors or middle powers in deploying military forces in protracted conflict situations. Thus coalitions of the willing have increasingly given way, or been replaced, by "coalitions of the willing and capable."

The most capable coalitions in deploying force are regional collective-defence and -security organizations. NATO's efforts to implement the Dayton accords to end Bosnia's civil war are the most prominent example of ad hoc collective peacekeeping by "coalitions of the capable." Although the United States and NATO countries were at the core of this coalition, through the Partnership for Peace mechanism, IFOR membership included a number of non-NATO European countries, notably Russia, whose involvement was viewed as crucial to the peace process. Four Islamic states — Egypt, Jordan, Malaysia, and Morocco — were also members. IFOR and SFOR also had unambiguous chains of command with authority ultimately residing in the Supreme Allied Commander Europe. IFOR was subsequently replaced by SFOR, but both operations had manifest unambiguous chapter VII authority provided by UN Security Council resolution 1031 to engage in peace enforcement as required.

The same cannot be said about the most recent NATO operation in Kosovo. Although the Security Council had called on Serbia to cease its military actions and withdraw its forces from Kosovo, it did not authorize bombing attacks or formal military action by NATO against Serbia. Although the international legal basis for NATO involvement in Kosovo is weak on three counts — first, because NATO is still, formally, an alliance based on the principle of self-defence; second, because the action is directed against a sovereign state that is dealing with a secessionist problem within its own borders; and third, because the UNSC has not given its formal blessing for such action — NATO has demonstrated that it can act. But there were obviously tensions that lay below the surface in spite of the brave front of Alliance unity. These tensions would have grown had there been a call to deploy ground forces in Kosovo.

If the new NATO marks a reinvigoration of the transatlantic partnership in this new post-Cold War environment, these recent missions by "coalitions of the capable" also underscore some of the real difficulties of collective and coordinated action when there are enormous disparities in the military capabilities of different coalition partners.

The need to improve the interoperability of forces among NATO and coalition partners is a continuing problem. Communications were a serious problem in the early days of IFOR's deployment in Bosnia because of equipment incompatibilities. Some of these problems were subsequently addressed but there remain major weaknesses in the sharing of data and information, communications, commonality of equipment, and the overall compatibility of systems.

The lengthy deployment of forces in Bosnia (first under IFOR and subsequently with the extension of SFOR's mandate) underscores the point that coalition-based operations can last for extended periods of time. The changing political timetable for such operations creates a real challenge for logistics as we saw in NATO air operations against Serbia.

Information systems are increasingly computer based. They are vulnerable to cyber-terrorists who can threaten infrastructure, power grids, and space-based communications systems. Some believe that this is the Achilles heel of modern armies. This may be the case, although some experts are more sanguine about these threats. But there is a need to focus on the methods, technologies, and approaches that can anticipate these new threats and reduce vulnerabilities of communications systems and databases. As the recent spate of bombings of American embassies and military barracks in Africa and the Middle East also reminds us, the terrorist threat is probably most acute for troops and personnel who are on the ground and deployed in hostile environments.

CONCLUSIONS

The following conclusions flow from the analysis presented in this chapter. First, the distinction between intrastate and interstate conflict is increasingly a blurry one. Recent interventions by the international community into so-called intrastate conflict have been prompted in part by humanitarian considerations but also by real concerns about the risks of escalation of these conflicts to the regional level. New technologies of warfare are also globalizing conflict processes as small states and regional powers acquire increasingly lethal technologies and long-distance delivery systems.

Second, when it comes to the use of military force either in peacekeeping, humanitarian, or enforcement operations, we are witnessing an important shift away from the UN to the increasing use of coalitions of the willing and capable. In the wider European theatre, the preferred institution of choice is NATO.

Third, there are important political issues associated with the subcontracting of military authority to regional collective-security or -defence mechanisms, such as NATO. If the Security Council is deadlocked and fails to offer its blessing, can these bodies act with any sort of political legitimacy?

Fourth, from an operational standpoint, there are important logistical, information, and interoperability issues associated with the effective deployment of military forces by coalitions of the capable. But in an environment where defence spending is falling and defence R&D budgets are being cut, it may be increasingly difficult to address these concerns.

REFERENCES

Axworthy, L. 1997. "Canada and Human Security: The Need for Leadership," *International Journal*, 52(2):183-96.

Boutros-Ghali, B. 1992. *An Agenda for Peace: Preventive Diplomacy, Peacemaking and Peace-Keeping. Report of the Secretary-General.* UN. GAOR/SCOR, 47th Sess., Preliminary List Item 10, at 55. UN Docs. A/47/277& S/24111.

Crocker, C.A. and F.O. Hampson (with P. Aall), eds. 1996. *Managing Global Chaos: Sources of and Responses to International Conflict.* Washington, DC: United States Institute of Peace Press.

Falkenrath, R.A. 1998. "Confronting Nuclear, Biological and Chemical Terrorism," *Survival*, 40(3):43-65.

Freedman, L. 1998. *The Revolution in Strategic Affairs*, Adelphi Paper No. 318. London: International Institute of Strategic Studies.

Hampson, F.O. 1989. "A Post-Modernist World: The Changing International Politico-Security System," in *Canada Among Nations/1988: The Tory Record*, ed. B.W. Tomlin and M. Appel Molot. Toronto: James Lorimer.

_____ 1996. *Nurturing Peace: Why Peace Settlements Succeed or Fail.* Washington, DC: United States Institute of Peace Press.

Orme, J. 1997/1998. "The Utility of Force in a World of Scarcity," *International Security*, 22(3):138-67.

Rotfeld, A.D. 1998. "Introduction: Transformation of the World Security System," in *SIPRI Yearbook 1998: Armaments, Disarmament and International Security*. Oxford: Oxford University Press.

Sisk, T.D. and D. Rothchild. 1997. "Beyond United Nations Peacekeeping: Changing International Responses to Intrastate Conflicts," paper delivered at the Annual Meeting of the American Political Science Association, Washington, DC, 28-31 August.

Sollenberg, M. and P. Wallensteen. 1998. "Major Armed Conflicts," in *SIPRI Yearbook 1998: Armaments, Disarmament and International Security*. Oxford: Oxford University Press.

Sprinzak, E. 1998. "The Great Superterrorism Scare," *Foreign Policy*, 112(Fall):110-24.

4

International Security and the RMA

S. Neil MacFarlane

INTRODUCTION

In this chapter, I examine the implications of the "revolution in military affairs" (RMA) for international security in the post-Cold War era. All analysts come to this subject with prejudices of one sort or another, as anyone who has read through the debate between the US Army and Air Force on the decisiveness or non-decisiveness of air power versus ground forces would be aware. I approach this topic from the perspective of someone who spends a good deal of time examining civil and low-level interstate conflict and multilateral responses to manage or resolve such conflict. This necessarily gives me an orientation somewhat different from someone who studies, for example, the implications of the RMA in interstate war between two major powers.

The topic of this chapter is central to the broader questions with which we are engaging in this volume; for an understanding of the RMA and of its relationship to modern conflict is essential to analysis and policymaking with regard to the restructuring of armed forces and defence industries and to the issue of how much of what to procure.

I begin by summarizing what I understand to be the RMA. I do not discuss whether recent and not so recent developments in military and associated technologies constitute a revolution — that is to say, rather than merely being an evolution of pre-existing methods and instruments, they constitute a transformative discontinuity in how we fight wars and how we think about them. That is an interesting topic, one well treated in the following chapter by Thierry Gongora.

Instead, I go on to examine briefly the claims that are made by proponents of these technologies and to examine what the Gulf War experience tells us about the validity of these claims. This is followed by a brief comment on international intervention in Somalia and Bosnia. I conclude with a number of observations on the "fit" between RMA technologies and contemporary conflict in the international system.

THE RMA

As to the basic characteristics of RMA technologies, the key lies in the development of information technology and notably miniaturization and processing of information (Freedman 1998, pp. 11-12, 21-22). I would note that in this sense the topic is a natural follow-up to the 1997 Canada-UK Colloquium, at Keele, which focused upon the social and economic impact of the communications revolution (Boyce 1999). Here we are looking in part at least at the military impact of a somewhat similar array of technological changes.

These technical developments have several important implications. One is a dramatic improvement in sensing capability. This provides policymakers, military planners, commanders, and also those in the field with greater quantities of more useful information about the capabilities and dispositions of the adversary and about their own dispositions at the strategic, operational, and tactical levels. The power of modern computers greatly enhances the speed at which this information can be processed. Associated developments in communications greatly increase the speed at which such information can usefully be disseminated to those who need to know. Processing and communications improvements also greatly enhance the capacity to integrate the various components of the military effort into a single "system of systems," combining air, sea, land, and very importantly, space operations.

Improvement in sensing and processing, in propulsion technologies, and in the miniaturization of guidance components has produced much more accurate weapons of much greater range. Stealth technology has greatly enhanced their capacity to penetrate the opponent's defences.

At this stage, it is important to note that these technical innovations and the interpretation of their strategic and tactical implications are rooted in Western societal attitudes toward war. The maturation of Western societies and the increasing complexity and interdependence of modern economies have made them much more vulnerable to disruption resulting from war damage. The abandonment of conscription and the professionalization of armed forces have reduced societies' capacities to deploy massive numbers of cannon fodder in battle. Declines in birth rates and the associated sensitivity to casualties in what Edward Luttwak has termed a "post-heroic age" (Luttwak 1996) have made societies less willing to tolerate large human losses. This effect is amplified by the consequently rising significance of a public opinion bombarded with near real-time media coverage. All of these conditions point in a certain direction when it comes to fighting wars. Lawrence Freedman summarizes the point as follows: "The series of developments that are brought together in the RMA have the connecting theme of the separation of the military from the civilian, of combatants from non-combatants, of fire from society, of organised violence from everyday life" (Freedman 1998, pp. 15, 17).

THE RMA AND THE GULF WAR

The claims of proponents of the RMA are well-known. They rest empirically in considerable measure on the first substantial conflict in which these capabilities were used on a large scale — the Persian Gulf conflict of 1990-91. (The second substantial conflict, the war with Serbia in 1999, occurred while this chapter was being drafted.) RMA advocates propose a vision whereby suitably equipped military establishments can collect, process, and disseminate information sufficient to deliver overwhelming force in a rapid and coordinated way over large distances, not only on the front line but to echeloned forces and strategic targets in the rear and with a minimum of collateral damage. The Gulf War appeared to confirm the existence of a qualitative transformation in the capacity to see the enemy, to analyze rapidly what we saw, and to act precisely, rapidly, and in a coordinated fashion on the basis of this intelligence. It produced quick and unambiguous victory with minimal casualties and little if any risk on the home front.

However, a closer glance suggests that we were not quite there yet in 1991. Intelligence was very good, but by no means complete. Weather played a significant role in limiting intelligence acquisition. Most of the satellite sensors could not penetrate cloud and the theatre was affected by low cloud over one-third of the time (McCausland 1993, p. 35). Target sets were, consequently, incomplete. For example, coalition sensors failed to identify the main Iraqi supply depot in Kuwait itself until it was actually captured. Sensing devices also proved to some extent to be susceptible to Iraqi efforts at deception. Intelligence for strategic targeting was also wrong on occasion, with disturbing consequences in terms of collateral damage, the most prominent example being the destruction of a bunker being used as shelter by large numbers of civilians.

One key constraint in the intelligence effort — not only for target identification but for more general intelligence tasks — was the lack of human assets on the ground in Iraq. This was a serious impediment in assessing the reliability of opposing Iraqi forces and the intentions of their commanders. The UK commander, General de la Billière, noted that "the coalition had no live assets in Baghdad due to the type of society it is. We could never assess accurately what sort of response we would get from the troops on the ground when the fighting started" (ibid.,

p. 57). Mechanisms for disseminating intelligence information to those who needed it on the ground were hampered by the concentration of intelligence assets at higher levels.

Damage assessment was also incomplete. This resulted in multiple insurance attacks. There were also problems in processing information received, with the production of imagery for interpreters lagging by days rather than hours. The bulk of the weaponry used was not smart but dumb. Nearly 90,000 tons of conventional munitions were dropped in the theatre in contrast to 6,250 tons of precision weapons (ibid., p. 29).

Some highly touted smart weapons such as the Patriot anti-missile defence system failed to handle their rather crude counterpart, the SCUD. As Jeff McCausland put it, low-tech was often difficult to defeat, presenting Western forces with serious problems. For example, the mine threat and the costs of reliably dealing with it were among several factors leading to the decision to forego an amphibious attack (ibid., p. 39). Meanwhile, the difficulties of tracking mobile SCUD launchers resulted in the commitment of substantial air assets to the search for them, drawing these assets off other important tasks. Ultimately, special forces infiltrated for ground reconnaissance made a significant contribution to the targeting of that limited number of SCUD mobile launchers that were actually destroyed.

In the last phase of the war, the point often made by proponents of ground forces proved true here as well. Air power cannot take and hold ground. To consummate the victory prepared by air and naval forces, it was necessary to break through ground defences, and to take and hold territory. This required a substantial deployment of heavy land forces.

Finally with regard to Iraq, it has often been pointed out that had Saddam Hussein actually set out to throw the RMA into a positive light, he could not have designed his strategy better. Iraqi forces lost command of the air very early on in the war. The Gulf War Air Power Survey noted that the result was "circumstances so ideal as to be the best that could be reasonably hoped for in any future conflict" (Watts 1993, p. 363). On the ground, meanwhile, the disposition of forces in lightly populated open spaces at a distance from urban centres permitted a war of manoeuvre that favoured highly mobile coalition forces relative to Iraqi units dug in fixed positions. Finally, had the Iraqis resorted to weapons of mass destruction (WMD), the entire picture would have been very different.

By way of summary, while the technologies associated with the RMA made a real difference, that difference was magnified by the adversary's lack of initiative at all levels, there were a number of serious weaknesses in the model, and the experience suggests that traditional capabilities retain essential importance even in a more or less ideal RMA environment. I have in mind human intelligence, special forces, and for that matter large ground formations. That said, the capabilities of traditional assets have been dramatically enhanced by RMA technologies.

POST-GULF WAR SCENARIOS

Operations in Somalia and Bosnia do provide some insight regarding the utility of RMA technologies in typical force contingencies of the post-Cold War era. The Somali operations involved not only the pacification of large stretches of countryside in order to facilitate humanitarian operations, but also the effort to secure highly unstable and heavily populated urban areas. They suggest that the RMA provides few answers on the intelligence side when operations are conducted against irregular forces in highly populated urban theatres. This was particularly evident in the incident involving US rangers deployed in October 1993 in an operation to capture Mohammed Aideed. In this instance, US forces were drawn into a disastrous tactical situation, producing casualties sufficient to ensure the withdrawal of the UN force as a whole, and causing a sea change in American attitudes toward participation in peace support operations on the ground. The case reinforced conclusions drawn from the Iraqi conflict with regard to the importance of traditional human intelligence capability, while underlining the limitations of these technologies in urbanized environments when those applying them were sensitive to the prospects for collateral damage.

The other obvious point to draw from the experience in Somalia is that it is difficult to translate massive military superiority into the attainment of political objectives. In this instance, the deployment of peacekeeping forces and the stabilization of the local situation was to be followed by negotiations leading to the re-establishment of effective government in Somalia and the reconstruction of that country. Peace forces stayed in Somalia in one form or another for over two years. There was (and is) no political settlement.

In the case of Bosnia, the bombing campaign in the summer and autumn of 1995, in which precision munitions were used to considerable effect against Serb targets with very limited collateral damage, has been cited as an illustration of the decisive impact of the air power version of the RMA in achieving desired results at low risk and low cost. Here, the obvious counter is that the successes of the Croats on the ground in Krajina and Slavonia were also significant in swaying Serb policy, as was the consolidation and hardening of UNPROFOR under General Rupert Smith into a real fighting force.

The renewal of international action against Saddam in December 1998 and the NATO action in Kosovo give us an opportunity to evaluate improvement in RMA technologies and their use in favourable conditions. In the first instance, the deck was stacked even more heavily in favour of the United States and Britain, since the forces acting against Iraq had access to the intelligence accumulated over the previous years by UNSCOM weapons inspectors. Confident conclusion regarding Desert Fox would be premature. However, it is noteworthy that early assessments suggest that there remain significant deficiencies. Pentagon analysts reported on the fourth day of the action that of the 97 targets hit during the first three days, only 28 were destroyed or heavily damaged, 46 were lightly or moderately damaged, and 23 had yet to be assessed.[1] Of the 27 SAM sites targeted in the initial stages of the action, it was reported that only one was destroyed, and only two seriously damaged

The NATO action in Kosovo that began in March 1999 also suggests that there has been little progress in addressing the problems with the RMA alluded to with regard to the Gulf War. Faulty intelligence remains a serious problem (*viz.*, NATO's destruction of the Chinese Embassy in Belgrade). The alliance has had difficulty in containing highly embarrassing collateral damage (*viz.,* damage to hospitals and attacks on buses and trains and tractors mistaken for tanks). The failure to suppress Serbian air-defence networks precluded low-altitude attacks that might have prevented these tragedies.

THE POST-COLD WAR THREAT ENVIRONMENT AND THE RMA

The above discussion raises a third issue: the relationship between perceived threats and RMA capabilities. The Gulf experience (and, for that matter, that of Kosovo) is atypical of the modern military environment, and, as noted, the peculiarities of the operational environment in the Gulf played to the advantages of the RMA. However, broadly speaking, the threats facing the US and other powers pursuing the RMA do not fit very closely with the high technology, combined arms, massive applications of force envisaged by RMA advocates. The RMA reflects in this sense its origins in consideration of how to cope with the Soviet military threat in Europe in the late 1970s and early 1980s without escalation to a nuclear war that would have destroyed what NATO was trying to defend. That is not a particularly credible contingency at the moment.

The current threat assessment is dominated by issues such as terrorism, drugs and international crime, economic migration, forced migration and related spillovers of small-scale conflict, and the proliferation of weapons of mass destruction, leaving aside the more diffuse discussion of economic and environmental security (INSS 1996, p. 211). Elements of the RMA are useful in attempting to cope with aspects of this agenda, but the package as a whole is not obviously relevant.

Moreover, the international agenda for the use of military assets by Western states since Iraq has been dominated not so much by set engagements between substantial state adversaries as by peace support operations. Again, RMA technologies may have considerable utility here, particularly in the area of intelligence and reconnaissaance. But multilateral organizations have limited intelligence capability of their own and face considerable difficulties in accessing the national intelligence resources of their members, for obvious reasons. In most instances, moreover, IFOR and SFOR being the quintessential examples, RMA capabilities appear to be supplements to, rather than replacements for, more traditional military capabilities.

A final observation returns us to our starting point. The RMA in its pure form was conceived for the prosecution of high-intensity war between states with substantial organized military forces and centralized hierarchical command and control. Such contingencies involving major states are, of course, possible. I agree with Fen Hampson that it would be unwise to ignore them. However, thus far in the post-Cold War era they are exceptional.

The more common variant of conflict involves communities as much as governments. It involves non-state actors as often as states. It occurs generally within societies rather than between states. Rather than exempting urban centres of population, they are often targets in ethnic cleansing. In other cases, units of the parties to conflict seek to take advantage of the tactical advantages of urban cover.

Fighters and fighting are intermingled with the civilian population. Many of those involved do not share the Western preference to dissociate war from the civilian population. Indeed, in many recent instances, as the former secretary-general of the UN, Boutros Boutros-Ghali, pointed out, the target in war is civilian (Boutros-Ghali 1995).

Much contemporary conflict relies on unsophisticated weapons systems that are not easily targeted by RMA technologies. To judge from Rwanda, and the level of casualties associated with the genocide that Britain and Canada (among others) tolerated, the most significant weapons innovation in the 1990s was not the movement of war into space, but the return of the machete.

The willingness to sacrifice and the tolerance of losses in the low-intensity wars of the 1990s has tended to be higher than the Western powers are comfortable with. It is also clear that in instances where conflict becomes internationalized, the parties understand the Western reluctance to take painful hits and understand also the utility of the media in taking advantage of this reluctance. The deliberate targeting, murder, and mutilation of Belgian members of UNAMIR in 1994 seems a good example of the former. The Rwandans wanted the Belgians out. They found a way to get what they wanted (Weiss and Collins 1996, p. 91). The treatment of the bodies of US rangers in Somalia is a good example of the latter.

The result appears to be, ironically, that as the means whereby we fight wars becomes more and more sophisticated, we appear to be less and less inclined to engage, except on terms that advantage our own way of war. But that does not appear to be the war that others want to fight.

NOTE

1. *International Herald Tribune*, 21 December 1998. Secretary of Defense William Cohen cautioned, however, against unduly pessimistic conclusions, noting that "when we make these preliminary assessments, what looks either to be light or moderate cannot be calibrated in terms of a normal understanding."

REFERENCES

Boutros-Ghali, B. 1995. "Supplement to An Agenda for Peace," in *An Agenda for Peace: Preventative Diplomacy, Peacemaking and Peace-Keeping.* New York: United Nations.

Boyce, R., ed. 1999. *The Communications Revolution at Work.* Kingston: School of Policy Studies, Queen's University.

Freedman, L. 1998. *The Revolution in Strategic Affairs*, Adelphi Paper No. 318. London: International Institute for Strategic Studies.

Institute for National Strategic Studies (INSS). 1996. *Strategic Assessment 1996: Instruments of U.S. Power.* Washington: National Defense University.

Luttwak, E. 1996. "A Post-Heroic Military Policy," *Foreign Affairs,* 75(4):33-44.

McCausland, J. 1993. *The Gulf Conflict: A Military Analysis*, Adelphi Paper No. 282. London: International Institute for Strategic Studies.

Watts, B. 1993. "Effects and Effectiveness," in *Gulf War Air Power Survey*, ed. E. Cohen. Washington: USGPO.

Weiss, T. and C. Collins. 1996. *Humanitarian Challenges and Intervention.* Boulder, CO: Westview Press.

5

The Shape of Things to Come: Sizing up the Revolution in Military Affairs

Thierry Gongora

INTRODUCTION

Although the notion that we are engaged in a "revolution in military affairs" (RMA) has gained tremendously in popularity since the Gulf War of 1991, there is still much debate about both its scope and its likely development. To make sense of the debate over this issue, it might be helpful to draw a distinction between a "military revolution" and the RMA (Murray 1997). The former term has been coined by military historians to refer to a transformation in the way states prepare for and wage war. Such a transformation has profound consequences for armies and the conduct of war, but it can also affect state and society, to the point of undermining an established social and political order. In truth, such military revolutions have been few and far between; since the late Middle Ages only a handful, three, perhaps four, of these kinds of transformation have occurred (Krause 1992, p. 22; Murray 1997, p. 73; Parker 1988, p. 146).

That being said, military historians have also found that other transformations in warfare, less drastic but still with significant impacts on armies and military operations, have occurred in larger numbers, particularly in the initial and maturing stages of a military revolution (Murray 1997, p. 73). One analyst has concluded that there have been ten of these periods of military innovation since the late Middle Ages (Krepinevich 1994). Such periods of military innovation yet not quite military revolution are today often called, retroactively, RMAs, primarily because of the current popularity of that rubric, but also because of the apparent need of some to try to find historical precedents to guide our thinking about current developments.

Thus, the military revolution initiated by the Napoleonic wars and the Industrial Revolution, which came to an apogee with the total wars of the twentieth century, included a series of smaller RMAs. Among them were the organizational innovations associated with the military victories of the French Revolution and Empire; the industrial and scientific innovations that yielded the railroad, modern artillery, and rifles so essential to the successes of the Union army during the American Civil War and of Prussia in the years 1866 to 1870; and during the twentieth century the Blitzkrieg, strategic bombardment, and the nuclear revolution.[1]

The distinction between a military revolution and an RMA has more than passing academic interest; establishing whether we are confronted by the former or the latter carries significant policy implications. If we are facing a military revolution, the policy debate should transcend issues of technology and operations to embrace such fundamental aspects of defence policy as the nature of future conflicts; the size, recruitment mode, and make-up of armed forces; the financing of defence; and the shape of the defence industrial base. Some writers also argue that military revolutions are phenomena of such scope that we are swept away by them, leaving us no recourse but to try to adapt to the new reality (Metz and Kievit 1995, pp. 9-10; Murray 1997, p. 72).

On the other hand, if we are only confronting an RMA, then the challenge becomes more manageable, and can be met within the current framework of defence, so long as the military maintain the ability to innovate (Rosen 1991; Watts and Murray 1996). The development of armoured warfare between the First and Second World Wars offers a classical case of how different states and their military establishments failed or succeeded in exploiting the potential of an RMA. While the Germans managed to field a significant armoured force by 1940, endowed with an appropriate doctrine and organization for its use, the French failed to use their armoured force in an efficient manner, while the British had too few adequate tanks to field a significant force initially, in spite of an early lead in the technology and theory of armoured warfare.

This chapter has the primary aim of assessing current changes in the military sphere in light of the above distinction between an RMA and a military revolution. In the following section, I address the nature and scope of the current RMA, as well as its likely development. Here I will argue that the RMA is driven by information technologies and that its path of development in the short- to medium-term future (i.e., the next 20 years) will be of an incremental nature: grafting information technologies on force structures and weapon systems, both being transformed only to the extent required by this process of integration.[2] A more radical transformation would require the emergence of a new type of weapon system, and of a military organization dedicated to its promotion; this has yet to occur. The section that follows explores the potential of the current transformation to turn into a full-fledged military revolution. The concluding section argues that although significant change is taking place in one of the fundamental elements of defence, namely the size and composition of armed forces, it is still premature to claim that we have entered an era of military revolution, because changes in other fundamental aspects of defence, especially financing and arms manufacturing, remain uncertain or limited. This conclusion is subject to revision, should change bite more deeply into the structure of defence in the future; this could happen if rivalries between major powers were to reach a level sufficient to trigger a new era of military competition favourable to military innovation.

THE CURRENT RMA: EVOLUTION IN THE REVOLUTION?

The technologies and operational concepts associated with the RMA are so numerous that one sometimes senses the term has become a marketing device, the defence industrial equivalent of the "cholesterol-free" and "high-fibre content" products the food industry likes to hawk. There are a plethora of RMA-related topics, ranging from missile defence to non-lethal weapons, from information warfare to dominant manoeuvre; no wonder the concept itself seems too mysterious for easy (or any) comprehension. At the risk of oversimplifying matters, I am going to impose some (arbitrary) conceptual order by focusing upon information technologies and their impact on military organizations and operations as the defining characteristics of the RMA. Even this may not be enough to ensure comprehension, for "information technology" itself is a vast domain, encompassing all those technologies that allow the gathering, transmission, and analysis of data — from satellites or AWACS to night goggles, laptop computers, and fax machines. When these technologies are integrated into a coherent system that includes modern weapons systems operated by highly trained personnel, they provide force multipliers to military formations allowing them to perform more complex manoeuvres, to fire accurately at longer range, and to experience a high degree of situational (including battlefield) awareness.

These technologies are not totally new; much of what we currently include under the rubric of the RMA has a precedent in military developments dating back to the 1970s and 1980s, or even to World War II (e.g., the British air-defence system during the Battle of Britain, and aircraft carrier operations in the Pacific). This does not detract from the significance of current changes, since an RMA requires decades to mature, and is rarely acknowledged to have happened until a war demonstrates its utlity (in this case, the 1991 Gulf War).

What is perhaps peculiar to the post-Gulf War period is that the information revolution is no longer confined to air warfare and naval operations. It increasingly affects land warfare, the environment that until now has remained the most difficult in terms of command and control of forces, performance of complex manoeuvres, detection of friendly and enemy units, and accurate fire (Freedman 1998, p. 12). Recent US efforts to integrate information technologies into the structure and equipment of ground units (the process of digitization) show impressive results despite the experimental nature of such formations.[3] In one exercise, performed in November 1997, a digital formation (the US 4th Infantry Division) showed that "[c]ompared with currently deployed forces, the digitized 4ID inflicted more than twice as many enemy casualties, in half the time, over three times the normal battlespace, using 25 per cent fewer combat platforms" (Hewish 1998). Such gains in "military productivity" are what Western armed forces will seek in the twenty-first century to make up for their decreasing size.

The potential of information technologies and the inventiveness of the human mind could theoretically lead to any number of outcomes for the RMA. Information technologies could spawn a system of defences that would dispense with the manoeuvre of heavily armed and protected forces in favour of a network of sensors linked to remote weapon platforms, able to fire smart munitions at long ranges. Such a scheme would be reminiscent of the "non-offensive defences" advocated by European critics of NATO conventional and nuclear rearmament during the 1980s.

In fact, such a system of sensors and light weapon platforms firing smart munitions is being considered to meet the requirements of the first element of a US expeditionary force in charge of securing a lodgement for the entry of subsequent forces (Hewish 1996). On a much grander scale, two American analysts have argued that the information technologies "brilliant munitions" (i.e., next-generation smart munitions) tandem will doom such large weapon systems as aircraft carriers, fighter bombers, and tanks, and will make possible the creation of a global strike system whereby the United States could strike any point on the planet in a timely and precise manner with weapons based in space or at home (Friedman and Friedman 1996).

Such futuristic schemes involving "reconnaissance-strike complexes," to use the term of the late Soviet military theorists who were the first to look at the current RMA, remain a remote possibility for the near- to medium-term future. The potential of information technologies is more likely to be grafted onto current forces and weapon systems than it is to evolve into completely new weaponry and operational concepts. There are several reasons for the expectation that incrementalism will characterize the RMA. Among them, we can cite bureaucratic and industrial interests, and the institutional legacy associated with the current forces and their weapon platforms. But military conservatism and entrenched interests do not tell the whole story. Given the limited amount of resources allocated to defence in the post-Cold War era, it is difficult to foster investment in totally new forces and weapon systems, given that these would have to be financed at the expense of the readiness and modernization of current forces, charged with the task of "holding the fort" during the transition period.

It is easier, therefore, for the RMA to be promoted as an exercise in the *upgrading* of late Cold War weapon systems and force structures than it is to pursue totally new and untried approaches. That being said, some resources will inevitably become diverted from the conventional war agenda that informs much of the initial RMA concept toward other tasks seen as more urgent in the current strategic environment, such as finding responses to the "asymmetrical" challenges to the RMA posed by weapons of mass destruction, terrorism, and protracted low-intensity conflicts.

An additional factor favouring the incremental path is that the strategic imperative to pursue an all-out exploitation of the potential of the RMA does not seem to be present. The United States already enjoys both a quantitative and qualitative conventional military edge over other powers. It certainly intends to use the RMA to maintain its qualitative edge, but it has no incentive to pursue the exploitation of the RMA along lines that would undermine the relevance of its current forces and their main weapon systems. Three RAND analysts have postulated this trio of alternative force postures for America's armed forces: conservatism (i.e., an emphasis upon the short run and an expectation of evolution); embracing the RMA; and tilting to the future, albeit cautiously (Davis, Gompert and Kugler 1997). It seems that this last option — prudent future tilt — comes closest to what is actually occurring today.[4]

Finally, the likely path of development for the RMA can be qualified as incremental, in the sense that it will improve traditional force structures and types of weapon platforms rather than *dispense with them* in favour of more radical solutions. It remains true, however, that from the standpoint of those in charge of integrating the information technologies into units, weapon systems, and operations, as well as of those who will operate them in the field, the challenges are great indeed, and do qualify as "revolutionary."

Despite its incremental development, the RMA remains a significant phenomenon that commands the attention of defence policymakers and analysts. This significance stems from the fact that the RMA affects all services and dimensions of military operations, and that the information technologies at its core have a similar impact on the economies and societies of advanced industrialized countries. The current RMA, therefore, seems broader in scope than such earlier twentieth-century RMAs as the Blitzkrieg, strategic bombardment, aircraft carrier operations, and the nuclear revolution, which were often more service or environment (air/sea/land) specific, and were not linked to similar developments affecting economies and societies.[5] Thus, there are grounds for considering that the current RMA might be a precursor to a vaster period of change that might qualify as a genuine military revolution.

WILL THE RMA LEAD TO A MILITARY REVOLUTION?

Having so far considered the RMA narrowly, as a military-technical revolution affecting armed forces, it is now time to switch gears and ask whether the observed changes will affect the broader parameters of defence policy. Military historians who have studied the relationship between military technology and war-making in Europe since the late Middle Ages have found evidence of a series of deep transformations in the way states prepare and wage wars over the centuries. These changes in war-making are called "military revolutions," and their impacts have been profound, shaping the emergence of the modern nation-state as well as the rise of Western dominion over the global system.

Can we glimpse in the contemporary period any signs of such a deep transformation? To answer this obliges an inquiry into the three fundamental elements of defence since the Renaissance (if not before): men, money, and weapons (or more broadly, matériel).[6] In other words, are there signs that the size and composition of armed forces are changing, along with the processes of arms manufacturing and the means of financing defence?

Past military revolutions have all been characterized by significant changes in the size and composition of armies. The decline of medieval warfare meant the demise of the small and élitist heavy cavalry, and its replacement by larger infantry formations supported by some cavalry and artillery; similarly, the decline of old-regime warfare was accompanied by the rise of the massive conscript armies of the French Revolution and of the Industrial Age. In this respect, the global trend in the size of armed forces in the most recent period (1985-96) indicates a significant decrease of 18 percent; although important regional disparities exist, with reductions of 26 percent and 14.5 percent for the NATO region and East Asia/Australasia, respectively, while the Middle East and sub-Saharan Africa have registered respective growth of 13 percent and 11.6 percent over the same period.[7]

Admittedly, some portion of these reductions and increases in the size of armies results from specific events such as the end of the Cold War in Europe, the aftermath of the Gulf War, and increased conflict and instability in sub-Saharan Africa. Nevertheless, the global decrease is significant for such a short period, and if it does last, or even intensify, this would represent an important development, particularly since sustained demographic growth implies that armed forces/ population ratios will also decline dramatically.

Perhaps as significant for defence policy making as the reduction in the size of armies is the transition from the conscript army model, inherited from the French Revolution and the world wars, toward more professional forces. This is hardly a novelty for the Anglo-Saxon world, but it is a major change for European continental powers like France, Germany, and Russia, for an Asian giant like China, or for a small nation-in-arms like Israel. The heightened reliance on active armed forces with a high proportion of professional troops at the expense of reserves and conscripts stems from the demands for increased competence and training required by modern combat operations, as well as for high readiness for quick deployment abroad. This trend toward smaller professional forces, however, seems to conflict with the recent operational requirement for extended peacekeeping operations. Prolonged peacekeeping operations tend to tax the limited personnel pool of professional armies, and to degrade their combat readiness. However, it remains to be seen whether the heightened operational requirement for peacekeeping is a passing trend linked to the early post-Cold War period, or a feature of the new strategic environment.[8]

Military revolutions in the past have also coincided with fundamental changes in weapons-production techniques (Krause 1992). For instance, advances in metallurgy that allowed the development of early artillery pieces were essential to the military revolution associated with the end of the Middle Ages and the beginning of the Renaissance (Rogers 1995, pp. 64-73). The powerful, mobile artillery thus created transformed war on land and sea in Europe, and paved the way for the European conquest of Asian states (Parker 1988, pp. 115-45). Similarly, the application of industrial-age techniques to the production of weapons and supplies allowed the fielding of mass armies from the second half of the nineteenth century on, and the waging of total wars thereafter.

Are we now on the threshold of a similar shift, one that would take us beyond the constraints of industrial-age weapons production? Some argue that recent developments in weapons production and military procurement do portend such change. Increased reliance on commercial off-the-shelf procurement, the effort to restructure defence production along the lines of the most innovative manufacturing/organizational practices in the private sector (what is called agile manufacturing), and the erosion of the civil/military industrial divide look propitious both for cost savings and for a shortening of the weapons-production cycle (Gansler 1997; Latham 1997).

But it remains unclear whether the parameters of industrial-age arms manufacturing have been transcended, especially when one considers mega-mergers in the aircraft/defence industry and continued cost overruns for many weapons programs. It is possible that all that the new production techniques will yield will be savings that can be applied against the cost of future acquisitions, without at the same time any halt, much less reversal, in the trend of increased cost for each new generation of weapons systems. It bears recalling in this regard that early in the twentieth century the Dreadnought class of battleships was built using new production techniques that yielded significant savings. Through its speed and firepower, the Dreadnought made obsolete all existing battleships, and all for an increase in price of only 10 percent; nevertheless the price tag of subsequent classes of battleships soared, and the total cost of acquiring a fleet based on such ships remained a significant burden on the defence budgets of Britain and Germany (Massie 1991). An upheaval in arms manufacturing is in progress, but only time will tell whether this will constitute a revolutionary transformation in the way we develop, produce, and procure weaponry.

The final point to consider in assessing the possibility of a military revolution concerns change in the way defence and military operations are financed. Each previous military revolution implied increased costs for procuring military power. The end of medieval warfare brought with it the need to pay for modern artillery, infantry, and warships, and to finance fortifications capable of withstanding the new artillery. Even the military revolution associated with the Industrial Revolution, which entailed significant savings in the production of weapons and supplies, raised the total cost of defence by allowing the fielding of larger forces, often supplied with more sophisticated equipment. As a result, statemakers through the ages have had to expend boundless ingenuity in financing defence and wars. Some states, such as the Netherlands and England, were so ingenious that they defeated the main European power of their age, respectively Hapsburg Spain and France, in prolonged conflicts. Similarly, in the twentieth century, the financing of the two global conflicts was a tremendous spur to the development of modern taxation and credit arrangements.

It is difficult to detect similar innovative developments in public finances today. The financial resources allocated to defence are so limited in some Western countries, Canada being a good example, that military power could be put in jeopardy if no re-engineering of forces were to take place.[9] Recent efforts to transform the administration of defence have been focused on the introduction of new management practices borrowed from the private sector. These practices are producing savings, but they will not be on a scale sufficient to finance the modernization of forces envisioned even by an incremental implementation of the RMA. The US example, arguably a large and wealthy defence establishment where great savings might be expected, demonstrates that private-sector "best practices" remain difficult to implement, are not necessarily applicable to the specific context of defence management, and may take time to produce savings, which will fall short of the financial requirements of defence modernization (Dahlman and Roll

1997; Khalilzad and Ochmanek 1997, p. 4). Improved efficiency in defence management is a worthwhile goal, and private-sector practices may help reach it in specific cases; but this administrative reform cannot provide a long-term solution to the financing of defence for advanced industrialized democracies living in an era of peace.

Outsourcing and outright privatization are fashionable trends that could lead to a significant development: a return of the "privatization" of violence and military services. Already in the past few years several security firms have made the headlines by providing military advice, and even conducting military operations (Shearer 1998). We should not take comfort from that trend. The historical record of military entrepreneurs and mercenaries is hardly a sterling one, except for the East India Company, which nevertheless expired with the Great Mutiny (1857-58). In fact, a singular accomplishment of modern public administration and of the professionalization of the officer corps has been the weeding out of profit, commercial schemes, and private business from the administration of armed forces.

Fortunately, the "new mercenarism" might not expand beyond a restricted niche, namely providing military advice to small or weak states. Therefore, there is little evidence that defence will be provided in the twenty-first century through other than the familiar methods. In fact, the pooling of resources through a long-term alliance may increasingly become the only affordable option. If this is the case, then the revolution in the financing of defence really started in 1949, with the creation of NATO.[10]

To sum up this section: a review of the fundamental indicators of a military revolution suggests that significant change is occurring in one indicator, the size and composition of armed forces; that some change, the extent of which is still uncertain, is taking place in weapons production; and that little change is noticeable in the way we finance defence, beyond the intensification of the established trend toward the international pooling of resources. In short, it is still premature to speak of a military revolution, but the evolution of these fundamental indicators in the future could lead to a reassessment. One must keep in mind that military revolutions are phenomena that take time to develop and, therefore, they are not as easily identifiable as the more quickly paced RMAs.

CONCLUSIONS

Ultimately, any assessment of the RMA, irrespective of whether it be "merely" a military-technical revolution or the beginning of a genuine military revolution, has to consider the most recurrent impetus for military innovation, that is, interstate rivalries. Without rivalries between states, military technology tends to stagnate. Recurrent conflicts between European powers from the Hundred Years War to the Cold War have had the unintended consequence of producing armies and weapons without parallel. In contrast, the great Asian empires of China, the Ottomans, or the Moguls relied on tradition-bound military systems to preserve order in their realms, with dramatic adverse consequences for imperial rule when the time came to confront Western powers.

In the case of the contemporary international system it is difficult to find, or foresee, a level of rivalry between major powers sufficient to trigger a spiral of insecurity, and thus usher in an age of boundless military innovation. The United States enjoys a clear edge in nearly all indicators of power, and most of the industrial and scientific resources needed to develop RMA-related military technologies are lodged in the American economy and other advanced economies whose states are allied to the US. Remaining challengers are either incomplete "peer competitors" such as Russia and China, which are unlikely to pose a global challenge for at least another ten years, or "niche competitors" such as India, Iran, a post-sanctions Iraq, and a reformed North Korea, powers that might challenge the United States on a regional basis, or compete with it in a few specific military technologies.

Moreover, the search for the next global military challenger to the United States assumes that cycles of hegemonic struggle, and their attending military revolutions or RMAs, are inevitable; this may no longer hold true. It is possible that the development of the international system has reached a stage at which war between major powers has become obsolete, as the resort to force in relations between states declines *pari passu* with the spread of democracy over the globe (Mueller 1989; Russett 1993).

As a result, it is likely that the RMA, though providing greatly improved armed forces, will in the end constitute an incremental process, one falling short of a true military revolution in the twenty-first century.

NOTES

1. The periodization and characterization of RMAs and military revolutions presented here are the author's own and are open to being debated; for instance, some scholars consider the French Revolution and the nuclear revolution to be military revolutions rather than RMAs.
2. Admittedly much of the following discussion is based on the distinction between "incremental" and "revolutionary" military technological change. An incremental innovation improves the performance of an existing weapon, while a revolutionary innovation introduces a new weapon and often makes some established weapons or military tactics obsolete; see Krause (1992, p. 22) for a similar distinction.
3. The performance of digital US Army units has been limited until now to military simulations and live exercises; in these live exercises the digital formation was supported by civilian technicians who dealt with the various information technologies

tested, and was confronted by an opposing force using the weapons and tactics of a "non-digital" Soviet-style formation.

4. Developments in the United States indicate that the RMA is implemented in an incremental fashion. Weapons systems that were radical departures from current systems have been cancelled (e.g., the Arsenal ship), while current main weapons platforms (such as tank, combat aircraft, attack helicopter, aircraft carrier, and submarine) keep being developed into more sophisticated versions rather than being rendered obsolete; plans for field unit reorganization in the US Army have fallen short of bold reform (Graham 1998); and DoD's official defence planning document (see Cohen 1997) is more conservative than an official panel of analysts would have liked it to be (see National Defense Panel 1997).

5. One could argue that strategic bombardment, the Blitzkrieg, and aircraft carrier operations were all sustained by a common technological revolution based on the radio and the internal-combustion engine, which also transformed economies and societies during the same period. This point underlines the fact that the periodization and definition of RMAs and military revolutions remain contentious issues.

6. These are recurrent themes in the literature on military revolutions; they also correspond to key elements of contemporary military policy according to Huntington (1961, pp. 1, 4).

7. Percentages calculated from figures taken from IISS (1997, p. 298).

8. Williams (1998, p. 16) shows that after a sharp rise in 1992-95 (a peak of 73,393 troops in 1994), the number of troops deployed in UN peacekeeping operations declined to a 1998 level (11,658 troops) approaching that of 1991 (9,314 troops). Similarly, the wave of armed conflicts that came in the aftermath of the Cold War, and that were at the origins of many large peacekeeping operations, has also been on the decline, from a high of 37 major armed conflicts in the world in 1990 to a total of 25 in 1997 (Sollenberg and Wallensteen 1998, p. 20).

9. The US experience, to the extent that it is generalizable, shows that force structure shrinks faster than defence expenditure; a 10-percent decrease in the defence budget can translate into 20 percent fewer combat units (Dahlman and Roll 1997, p. 273; Davis and Kugler 1997, pp. 102, 133).

10. While the pooling of resources for defence at the origins of NATO can be seen as threat-driven — i.e., the desire to create a large and cohesive bloc to deter the Soviet Union — the current and future pooling of resources is driven by the inability of many states to afford key defence equipments such as satellites, airborne radars, long-range logistical assets, and a diversified defence industry on a national basis.

REFERENCES

Cohen, W.S. 1997. *Report of the Quadrennial Defense Review.* Washington, DC: Department of Defense. www.dtic.mil/defenselink/pubs/qdr.

Dahlman, C.J., and C.R. Roll. 1997. "Trading Butter for Guns: Managing Infrastructure Reductions," in *Strategic Appraisal 1997: Strategy and Defense Planning for the 21st Century,* ed. Z.M. Khalilzad and D.A. Ochmanek. Santa Monica, CA: RAND Corp.

Davis, P.K. and R.L. Kugler. 1997. "New Principles for Force Sizing," in *Strategic Appraisal 1997: Strategy and Defense Planning for the 21st Century,* ed. Z.M. Khalilzad and D.A. Ochmanek. Santa Monica, CA: RAND Corp.

Davis, P.K., D. Gompert and R.L. Kugler. 1997. "Adaptiveness in Defense Planning: The Basis of a New Framework," in *Strategic Appraisal 1997: Strategy and Defense Planning for the 21st Century,* ed. Z.M. Khalilzad and D.A. Ochmanek. Santa Monica, CA: RAND Corp.

Freedman, L. 1998. *The Revolution in Strategic Affairs,* Adelphi Paper No. 318. London: Oxford University Press/International Institute for Strategic Studies.

Friedman, G. and M. Friedman. 1996. *The Future of War: Power, Technology, and American World Dominance in the 21st Century.* New York: Crown Publishers.

Gansler, J. 1997. "Transforming the Defense Industrial Base to Match the Revolution in Military Affairs: An American Perspective," unpublished paper.

Graham, B. 1998. "Army Plans Modest Makeover of Combat Divisions," *Washington Post,* 9 June, p. A1. http://208.134.241.211/wp-srv/WPlate/1998-06/09/0381-060998-idx.html.

Hewish, M. 1996. "At the Sword's Point: Specialized Equipment for Early-Entry Forces," *International Defense Review,* 29(11):36-43.

_____ 1998. "US Army Marches Towards a Digital Horizon," *International Defense Review,* 31(1):11.

Huntington, S.P. 1961. *The Common Defense: Strategic Programs in National Politics.* New York: Columbia University Press.

International Institute of Strategic Studies (IISS). 1997. *The Military Balance 1997/98.* London: IISS/Oxford University Press.

Khalilzad, Z.M. and D.A. Ochmanek. 1997. "Introduction," in *Strategic Appraisal 1997: Strategy and Defense Planning for the 21st Century,* ed. Z.M. Khalilzad and D.A. Ochmanek. Santa Monica, CA: RAND Corp.

Krause, K. 1992. *Arms and the State: Patterns of Military Production and Trade.* Cambridge: Cambridge University Press.

Krepinevich, A.F. 1994. "Cavalry to Computer: The Pattern of Military Revolutions," *The National Interest,* 37(Fall):30-49.

Latham, A. 1997. "The Contemporary Restructuring of the US Arms Industry: Toward 'Agile Manufacturing'," *Contemporary Security Policy,* 18(1):109-34.

Massie, R.K. 1991. *Dreadnought: Britain, Germany, and the Coming of the Great War.* New York: Ballantine Books.

Metz, S. and J. Kievit. 1995. *Strategy and the Revolution in Military Affairs: From Theory to Policy.* Carlisle Barracks, PA: U.S. Army War College, Strategic Studies Institute.

Mueller, J. 1989. *Retreat from Doomsday: The Obsolescence of Major War.* New York: Basic Books.

Murray, W. 1997. "Thinking about Revolutions in Military Affairs," *Joint Force Quarterly* (Summer):69-76. www.dtic.mil/doctrine/jel/jfq_pubs/1416pgs.pdf.

National Defense Panel. 1997. *Transforming Defense: National Security in the 21st Century.* Washington, DC: National Defense Panel. www.dtic.mil/ndp/FullDoc.pdf.

Parker, G. 1988. *The Military Revolution: Military Innovation and the Rise of the West, 1500-1800.* Cambridge: Cambridge University Press.

Rogers, C. 1995. "The Military Revolutions of the Hundred Years War," in *The Military Revolution Debate: Readings on the Military Transformation of Early Modern Europe,* ed. C. Rogers. Boulder, CO: Westview Press.

Rosen, S.P. 1991. *Winning the Next War: Innovation and the Modern Military.* Ithaca, NY: Cornell University Press.

Russett, B. 1993. *Grasping the Democratic Peace: Principles for a Post-Cold War World.* Princeton, NJ: Princeton University Press.

Shearer, D. 1998. *Private Armies and Military Intervention,* Adelphi Paper No. 316. London: IISS/Oxford University Press.

Sollenberg, M. and P. Wallensteen. 1998. "Major Armed Conflict," in *SIPRI Yearbook 1998: Armaments, Disarmament and International Security.* Oxford: Oxford University Press/SIPRI.

Watts, B. and W. Murray. 1996. "Military Innovation in Peacetime," in *Military Innovation in the Interwar Period,* ed. W. Murray and A.R. Millett. Cambridge: Cambridge University Press.

Williams, M.C. 1998. *Civil-Military Relations and Peacekeeping,* Adelphi Paper No. 321. London: IISS/Oxford University Press.

Part Two

DEFENCE INDUSTRIAL STRUCTURE

6

Globalization Meets the Defence Industry

Sir Geoffrey Pattie

INTRODUCTION

It would seem that the term "globalization" is the buzzword of the moment. We read and hear constantly about the globalization of the marketplace, the globalization of industry, the global revolution in telecommunications, but what exactly do we mean by this word? Can we concoct some acceptable definition of the term globalization? Can an activity be internationalized but not be globalized?

Since I am a businessman and not an academic, I will choose in this chapter to concentrate on the realities facing the defence industry today, on the rapid changes and initiatives that have taken place over the last few years and months at both the national and international levels, and to explore whether the defence industry can ever become a truly globalized activity. It is perhaps best in the first instance, however, to begin by trying to define what we mean by the term *globalization*, and then to move on to a brief history of the phenomenon.

I would propose the following definition: a process in which the constraints of geography on economic, political, social, and cultural arrangements recede and in which people become increasingly aware that they are receding. For many industrial activities this is the case, but the paradox for the aerospace and defence industry as a whole, is that it is internationalized, but *not* globalized. In what follows I will endeavour to explain the reasons why, and to explore the possibilities for globalization. Before doing so, it is important that I explore, briefly, the historical development of globalization.

THE HISTORICAL DEVELOPMENT OF GLOBALIZATION

Globalization is about people and process; the spread of business and changed practices; and the ability of these factors to create links that will break down political frontiers. Perhaps the earliest activities to make the assault on such barriers were religion, the spread of Christianity for example, and economics, as trading between countries began. Modern globalization is driven by economics and, as the world financial markets are interlinked and interdependent, frontiers are transcended. Two of the earliest multinational businesses to emerge were close to home for Canadians: the Hudson's Bay Trading Company, which in the late nineteenth century was the world's first truly multinational company, and the enterprise of one Hiram Walker, who set up a distillery in Windsor, Ontario, in the 1850s.

In the late nineteenth century organizational and technical innovations helped companies to a much larger scale of production, while rapid changes in domestic and international transport, communications, and storage techniques helped to create new market opportunities. These developments gave industry the ability to acquire property rights and therefore produce on a much larger scale, providing opportunities to become multi-product, and multinational. From that point onwards modern globalism has become driven by economics and has transcended the frontiers of the nation-state. The period 1910 to 1945 and the post-World War II economic environment saw an explosion of economic activity and the advent of branded goods. In addition, the Bretton Woods system was critical to the development of global economic reorganization, attempting to strike a balance between a liberal world market and the domestic responsibilities of states. States became accountable to the newly created agencies of an international economic order such as the International Monetary Fund, the World Bank, and the General Agreement on Tariffs and Trade. Perhaps one can even go so far as to say that today's values of globalism are the values of North American capitalism

Globalism today is much broader than ever before, as we witness the "sharing" of international events through high-tech communications and financial interdependency, which determines outcomes in world financial markets. For example, the collapse of the Asian "tiger" economies in 1997 not only directly affected the states themselves, sending them into a downward spiral of recession and depression, but the global economy too, as we appeared to be heading toward global recession in its wake. Perhaps the classic example of industrial globalization today is Microsoft *Windows*, whose use defines most business environments. The Internet is an even more interesting example of globalization; it has no frontiers, and there is little if any national governmental control.

WHY HAS THE DEFENCE INDUSTRY TRADITIONALLY ESCAPED GLOBALIZATION?

It was not until the 1890s that defence technology and its base became recognized as a vital national asset. Governments grew aware that technical edge and an advantage in production were vital to a state's armed capability. National "defence industrial bases" developed as relations with the armed forces strengthened, and governments began to encourage technological innovation.

In the 1960s, as the costs of research and development began to rise, international cooperation in defence technology did begin to develop as some European countries were prepared to trade a modicum of independence in this field to have access to these developing technologies. France remained the exception. But, by the late 1960s the European defence industrial base had begun to break down, and any collaboration was on a project-by-project basis while core collaboration atrophied.

The words "national" and "sovereignty" are the key to understanding why the defence industry is paradoxically internationalized but not globalized. Defence is a matter of national security and therefore until now there has been no free market applied to it. A broadly based national military production capability is critical to national security. It is argued that dependence on non-national defence systems increases the vulnerability to foreign pressure. Even with the European Union, the member states have always referred to article 223 of the Treaty of Rome, which states that:

(a) no Member State shall be obliged to supply information the disclosure of which it considers contrary to the essential interests of its security;

(b) any Member State may take such measures as it considers necessary for the protection of the essential interests of its security which are connected with the production of or trade in arms, munitions and war material; such measures shall not adversely affect the conditions of competition in the common market regarding products which are not intended for military purposes.

Article 223 has been invoked by the member states on many occasions, even in respect of the protection of army socks!

GLOBALIZATION OF THE DEFENCE INDUSTRY TODAY?

As noted above, the paradox is that the defence industry is internationalized but not globalized. Before turning to this industry's possible consolidation and globalization, perhaps we should consider for a moment what we mean by "globalization." Do we in fact mean something else? Do we mean "regionalization" in the sense of "Europeanization," or "South Africanization," or even "Canadianization"? The current debate in Europe is most surely about the Europeanization, *not* the globalization, of defence. At present in Europe our security community is NATO, but for the United States NATO is only one part of its security community. By creating a common European defence policy with its organizational structures we will in fact be creating yet another security community. At the heart of the European debate is the question as to whether individual countries will be prepared to pool their representative and operational sovereignty without abandoning themselves to a common security policy.

Economic circumstances are driving the restructuring issue in Europe, as defence spending has fallen by 25 percent in real terms between 1984-85 and 1994-95, with the equipment portion declining from 45 percent to 40 percent over the same period. These shrinking defence budgets and national markets, increased competition, and exponential increases in the costs of developing new weapons due to the rapidity of technical change have been forcing the debate on the rationalization and restructuring of the European defence industry, challenging the long-held view that the defence industry cannot be globalized, or "Europeanized." Add to these problems the disengagement of governments as the threat has decreased, no longer providing the financial safety blanket they once did, the rapid pace of consolidation in the United States and simple "peer pressure," the European defence industrial complex has been forced to recognize that the world has changed and consequently some radical changes are required in its own structures.

When the heads of state and government of France, Germany, and the United Kingdom made their now famous Trilateral Agreement of November 1997, they were acknowledging that there is a need in Europe for an efficient and globally competitive European aerospace and defence electronics industry. Their conclusions were that it would "help to improve Europe's position in the global market, promote European security, and ensure that Europe will play a full role in its own defence."

There is an irony here, however; the reality that there is no longer a single enemy in a defined theatre of operation makes intergovernmental program cooperation more difficult, even as budgetary pressures make it more necessary. It also begs the question as to which comes first: the policy or the consolidation?

In fact, industry itself was already beginning to seek solutions to the problems that the three leaders were articulating. The surprise was that the latter set a deadline of 31 March 1998 for the industry to present a restructuring plan, and that there was no acknowledgement of the restructuring that had already begun to take place.

The benefits of consolidation were, and remain, obvious to the industry. European businesses began their own initiatives long before the tripartite announcement of November 1997, recognizing the increased competitiveness from the US, where the industry had already moved quickly in response to the changed market and consolidated itself into three huge conglomerates. However, one should add that the Department of Defense (DoD) has also helped in this process by reimbursing defence contractors for a portion of the costs involved in mergers, and by waging a successful campaign to have the antitrust rules lifted. Apart from this obvious point of making the European defence industry more competitive, there are manufacturing economies of scale to be considered, the advantage of greater marketing muscle, the advantages of cross-sector synergies which are available to consolidated companies, and reduced overlapping of research and development, therefore giving a greater return from research and development funding. However, to keep matters in proportion, we must bear in mind that in 1998 alone the American research and development budget exceeded the total defence budget of Germany!

The US defence industries recognized the new market realities earlier than did their European counterparts and have steamed ahead at breathtaking speed in their efforts to consolidate. But even for Washington there does appear to be a limit beyond which it will not allow further consolidation. The rejection of the proposed Lockheed-Martin/Northrup-Grumman merger signalled the Clinton administration's fears of the increasing lack of domestic competition this link-up would bring ("Merger Timeout" 1998). By contrast, as already noted, the more ponderous European approach results from the notion of sovereignty. Individual governments feel that a broadly based military production capability is critical to national security. They are also concerned about the impact of restructuring upon the industry's workforce with the inevitable redundancies that will ensue. Some governments fear foreign ownership, and some desire to protect their industries without regard for profit. It is little wonder that the European approach is far more cautious and much slower.

The swift unification of the American market, contrasted with the fractured European defence market, is already beginning to exaggerate the differences that have always existed, primarily with respect to research and development. The technological gap is widening, and fast. There is real fear that the European militaries will soon not be able to interoperate unless they purchase US systems. This will put the Atlantic alliance under severe pressure.

THE EUROPEAN RESPONSE: DEVELOPMENTS SO FAR

During the past two years in Europe there have been a number of significant developments. In November 1997 the EU Commissioner responsible for industry

(DG3) produced a paper on "The Restructuring of the European Defence Industries." There are many who feel that in this paper Commissioner Bangemann strayed far beyond his competences with proposals aiming for a single market in defence and, therefore, a common defence policy. Bangemann's paper is still very much in play, although it was overshadowed later that November by the above-mentioned tripartite agreement.

In the summer of 1998, there was a flurry of activity both on the industrial and political fronts, the general intent of which was to stimulate consolidation. In the early summer, the British government issued its long awaited Srategic Defence Review (SDR), which announced the streamlining of Britain's procurement organization and procedures, taking into account the pace of industrial change and industrial consolidation. This was quickly followed by the signing of a letter of intent on *"Measures to Facilitate the Restructuring of the European Defence Industry,"* by the defence ministers of the original three — France, Germany, and the UK — joined now by their Italian, Spanish, and Swedish counterparts.

Later in July, France, which had been the country holding back on its industry restructuring plans because of government ownership and support of much of the industry, took a step forward. The Socialist government announced the acquisition by the state-owned Aérospatiale of the defence interests of Matra, part of the Lagardère group. This was seen to constitute the partial privatization of Aérospatiale, since Lagardère took a share of 30 to 33 percent. Up to a further 20 percent is to be sold on the stock market, leaving the French government with the remaining 46 to 48 percent of the shares.

Since the summer of 1997, and especially during 1998, events moved apace, as each day brought more news of change in defence industrial arrangements. By the early autumn of 1998 it was possible to discern some significant events at the European Union (EU) level, which were bound to nudge the consolidation process further along. The British government was very busy during this period. Prime Minister Blair quietly initiated a review of Britain's role in the EU, mindful of the image of the country as being "bad Europeans." The review was conducted to determine if there was any area in which the United Kingdom could play a leading and constructive role. There was: defence policy. The UK wanted to help "beef up" European defence capabilities without undermining NATO's preeminence. This objective continues to be important, all the more so in the wake of the war with Serbia in the spring of 1999.

CONCLUSIONS

The need for the consolidation of the European defence industry has been put in the starkest of terms by the British secretary of state for defence, George Robertson, echoing the American debate: "consolidate or die." If the UK and indeed other European countries lose out to US competition in the emerging markets of Central and Eastern Europe and the Pacific Rim, then orders from the domestic markets will not be enough to sustain them.

Whatever the outcome of the restructuring of the European defence business, my own company (GEC) has started to look across the Atlantic; we have recently acquired the American company Tracor, adding to our Marconi North America operations, while we already own Canadian Marconi. Perhaps we are now witnessing the globalization of defence after all. Certainly, if the EU does get its wish then there will be no doubt in my mind.

In the meantime, GEC believes that it is essential for the defence industry to face both ways and not witness the development of "fortress Europe." In the long run, the only basis on which the defence industry can flourish is through achieving far greater efficiency and, thereby, sufficient commercial terms to meet investor expectations and investment needs. GEC therefore does not consider the integration of the European industry to be an end in itself, but merely one of a number of means to achieve productivity and other performance gains comparable to those under way in the United States. As industrialists, we should be striving to create businesses that can match and compete with their American counterparts, and to harmonize European efforts to collaborate along the whole range of the procurement cycle. And, as industrialists, we should never lose sight of the fact that we must produce value for our shareholders.

REFERENCE

"Merger Timeout." 1998. *Washington Post*, 25 March, p. A20.

7

Transatlanticism versus Regional Consolidation

Trevor Taylor

INTRODUCTION

We live in interesting times as far as armaments in NATO are concerned. The United States is threatening to push ahead with a "revolution in military affairs" (RMA), in part by equipping its forces extensively on information-based systems. There is a limited but persistent interest, in Washington and elsewhere, in ballistic missile defence systems that would demand extensive funding and increased integration of defence in Europe. There is uncertainty in the US about whether the defence industrial scene will be dominated by three or four companies, while in Europe there is at least the possibility that major transnational defence companies (or even one dominant transnational company) will shortly be formed. Such an entity or entities, to be able to organize and operate efficiently, will need major increases in the cooperative behaviour of governments. There is also a mass of cooperative and collaborative activity in the armaments area, but much of it appears in some disarray. Finally, NATO's governments have recently unveiled a new Strategic Concept, elaborating upon the long-term purposes of the alliance. It must be asked whether the alliance could flourish if the transatlantic defence industrial scene were to be completely dominated by competitive, adversarial relationships, or if European defence businesses were overtly subservient to those of the US.

It needs to be stressed from the outset that regional consolidation in Europe's defence industry is quite compatible with transatlantic links; indeed, it holds out the possibility of partnership between firms of roughly equal status. However, especially now that Washington has engineered the reduction of its defence prime contractors to three giant players, transatlanticism without European consolidation can only mean America's technological and economic domination of the NATO arms market.

In the light of the above, this chapter explores the future of intra-European and transatlantic armaments collaboration. Collaboration I define as a shared effort by two or more states to develop and produce new equipment. Collaboration is thus a particular case of arms cooperation. The latter can involve a range of other activities including simple trade, licensed production, and offset arrangements.

THE COLLABORATIVE BARGAIN

Decisions to collaborate can be driven by several considerations, including political ones. In the 1960s, Britain was keen to stress its European credentials and used arms projects with France and Germany for this purpose. In the 1990s, it can be maintained that there exists a British aspiration to show that collaboration with the US is desired and can be successful. This is at least one element behind the Tracer project and even the United Kingdom's role in the Joint Strike Fighter (JSF) program: these efforts could be unkindly described as reflecting the triumph of hope over experience. But, beyond politics, defence collaboration is predominantly concerned with the economic dimension.

Collaboration is usually based on expected savings derived from the sharing of fixed costs. However, joint projects in Europe have rarely been based on simple foundations. Indeed they have often reflected a wider bargain in which all parties submitted technology, finance, and access to their markets. In addition, they shared out technological risk while seeking to contain the increased political risk within moderate limits. Arrangements in which all parties submitted an equal share in each dimension appeared easiest to foster, but countries that fell short on one dimension could make good elsewhere. Spain was not in a position to contribute 13 percent of the technology for the Eurofighter without external help, but it was welcome as a partner because of the money it was ready to advance and the market it would provide.

Having put their share of technology, money, and market into the pot, collaborative partners hoped to take an appropriate mix from it in the form of jobs, technological expertise, and even defence equipment. Within Europe, collaborative projects have been concerned with security, jobs, technology, foreign exchange, prestige, and foreign policy options from defence procurement. Even when national projects could not be justified in financial terms, the collaborative route was often preferred to buying from the US.

EUROPEAN COLLABORATIVE EXPERIENCE TO DATE

To gain some clues about the future, it is helpful to glance at the past. Western Europeans, and especially France, Germany, and the UK, have almost 40 years of experience with collaborative projects. Projects such as the Franco-German Alphajet and the Milan-HOT-Roland missiles date back to the early 1960s. In the same decade, Britain and France were linked by the Jaguar aircraft and by the Puma-Lynx-Gazelle group of helicopters. Many of the early projects were driven by political rather than military or even economic considerations, but that did not prevent them from being military and even commercial successes.

All projects have operated on the basis of *juste retour*, the idea that a state's share of the partners' total demand should determine its contribution to development and production costs and its share of research and development (R&D) and production work. There has been increasing dissatisfaction, especially in Britain, Germany, and even France, with the *juste retour* principle. It can mean that non-competitive companies are awarded contracts just so that their state can have its specified work share. When, as has happened with the Typhoon (formerly Eurofighter), the principle has been applied to subsystems and sub-subsystems, development has been delayed as companies have needed time to find appropriate partner firms in each of the participating countries (Natural Audit Office 1995, para. 2.3).

Collaborative projects have been managed in various ways. Occasionally one government has been given the clear lead, as was the case with France and the Alphajet. More frequently, however, projects have been managed on the governmental side by an international agency (i.e., a committee of the participating governments). The agency has interacted on the contractors' side with a specially created joint venture (JV), such as Eurofighter GmbH. Such JVs have not been given much power or autonomy by their member companies, and so essentially a committee of governments has dealt with a committee of companies. The limitations of this practice too have become apparent in terms of the delays in decision making that can result.

Normally, governments have established extensive national project management groups behind the international agencies. Governments have run collaborative projects on a national basis as well as jointly in other ways. In particular, national approvals procedures have been used to allow a project to proceed from one phase to another and, in Germany in particular, the legislature has to authorize financial support for projects at the different stages. The need for national approvals at different stages has meant that collaborative projects have often been marked by notable delay, because they have been able to proceed only at the speed of the slowest player. Expectations about the anticipated slow development speed of a next generation communications satellite system led the UK to withdraw from the project in 1998. The proposed Future Large Aircraft and Next Generation Frigate cannot advance in the face of national hesitation on the part of one or more partners.

National reviews and indecision have predictably affected collaborative projects, particularly since the end of the Cold War. The partners in any collaborative venture do not necessarily give it equal priority. In 1989, the fact that two or more states had a "requirement" for a system did not mean that they wanted it equally badly. When political circumstances change drastically, countries can be expected to have different ideas about the specific systems that they will want to abandon or keep.

After 1990, European states varied in how they adjusted both their overall defence spending and their foreign and security policies. These amendments had an impact on which collaborative projects became delayed, and even survived or failed. The Eurofighter/Typhoon was delayed but survived, as did the NH-90 and the Tiger helicopters. Britain lost interest in the long-range Trigat missile and France was unable to persuade Germany to invest in reconnaissance satellites. With a Social Democrat-led government being elected in Germany in 1998, the Anglo-German-French armoured troop carrier, the "battlefield taxi," has apparently gone into a phase of suspended animation while the Schröder government ponders whether it really wants such a vehicle. Overall, as the 1990s draw to an end, it is difficult to identify many major European collaborative projects that have actually come into service since the previous decade. The Anglo-Italian Merlin antisubmarine helicopter looks to be a rare exception, and should be in service with the Royal Navy in 1999.

Several European governments have become progressively dissatisfied with the traditional ways of making collaborative projects work (or, as the case may be, *not* work). As long ago as 1986 the then Independent European Program Group (IEPG) states endorsed the findings of the Vredeling report recommending, among other things, the end of *juste retour* arrangements on individual projects. It was suggested that work shares on bundles of projects might be monitored and adjusted. In practice, however, states still look for a suitable work share from each project. France, for instance, may not participate in the future battlefield taxi,[1] because it believes Giat has an inadequate work allocation.

However, the bundling of projects is a useful accounting exercise that could well be taken up by the four-member Organisation conjointe de coopération en matière d'armement (OCCAR), an organization whose legal identity should be established in 1999 when Britain, France, Germany, and Italy ratify the agreement they signed in September 1998. In principle, OCCAR could even become a procurement agency, contracting and managing projects on behalf of governments.

Thus, collaboration in Europe has a very mixed record and reputation. Keith Hartley's calculation that, on average, collaborative projects take even longer to execute than national projects must still be valid. However, it cannot be proven that any particular project would have been executed more quickly as a national project. History cannot be rerun. Earlier in this decade, the British national Phoenix reconnaissance drone was significantly over-budget and late. Had it been a collaborative effort, the availability of a larger pool of engineering intelligence might have meant that it could have been brought into service more quickly. Moreover, the limitations of the collaborative process have not prevented governments turning to it. Indeed, the UK is on course to have 40 percent of its equipment spending tied up in collaborative projects before long. Most of these involve European states, although, as noted, there have been some significant transatlantic endeavours.

THE RECORD OF TRANSATLANTIC COLLABORATION

There was no real effort to promote transatlantic defence collaboration until the latter part of the 1970s. At this stage, there was a growing interest in NATO standardization, rationalization, and interoperability as part of the concern to see the West's conventional forces carry a greater share of the deterrence burden. There were extensive discussions about the "two-way street" and the American reluctance to buy European defence equipment. Under President Carter, then US armaments director William Perry advanced the idea of "families of weapons." The US would lead the development of one family member, the Europeans another. Both sides would buy the finished products from each other.

There was a commitment to try this first in air-to-air missiles, with the US developing the Advanced Medium Range Air-to-Air Missile (AMRAAM) and Europeans a short-range version of the weapon (ASRAAM). Many Europeans doubted that the US Air Force would accept reliance on a European system for such an important weapon, and France went ahead with its own missile, the MICA, to serve both short- and medium-range roles. There was concern in Europe that the US could have used its control over the export of AMRAAM to restrict the sale of European aircraft that would need to carry it. After the European developers neglected the concerns of the US about the ASRAAM's integration onto existing aircraft, the US in fact did proceed with its own short-range program, yet another version of the AIM-9 Sidewinder, and Germany later dropped out of the ASRAAM program. The latter weapon is being completed, but as a UK national project, and has been procured by Australia for its F-18s.

Since Perry's initiative, transatlantic armaments programs have been, to adapt Norman Augustine's phrase, "unblemished by success." A possible exception has been the AV-8B VSTOL combat aircraft, which was nominally a US-British development of the original Harrier. The US did pass along useful technology on Harrier avionics to British Aerospace (BAe), and the sales to the US, plus related exports to Spain and Italy, helped BAe to enjoy about 40 years of production work on the different variants of the aircraft. However, the AV-8B was essentially a US-dominated program, and McDonnell Douglas did not share its wing technology on the aircraft.

There is little doubt that the US side must bear the major responsibility for the negative record of transatlantic equipment collaboration. Economically and even technologically, the US has largely not needed to collaborate, as its own defence budget, technology base, and arms market have been large enough to justify domestic-only programs.

Politically, in the defence procurement area, Washington constitutes not a single government but rather comprises three sets of actors, each enjoying considerable independence. There is the administration, led in defence by senior members of the Office of the Secretary of Defense. There is Congress, which provides money on an annual basis for individual weapons programs. Finally, there are the (four) individual services that have the central responsibility for selecting their defence equipment. A successful collaborative project would require consistent, long-term support from all three of these governmental actors.

Moreover, the US as a whole has not been willing to practise the give-and-take that Europeans know is necessary if collaboration is to succeed. In order to make *juste retour* work, and to give all parties the technology access they want, European collaborative projects have often been marked by the relatively free exchange of technology. The US refuses to countenance such free exchanges, maintaining instead a restrictive technology-transfer control mechanism in the Pentagon and State Department.[2] Linked to this, Europeans basically operate on the expectation that any partner in a collaborative project may export that project to any customer it considers suitable. In addition, the European Union states are working toward a common arms-export policy and have agreed to a common Code of Conduct on arms exports. The US insists on a veto right regarding the re-export of its defence technology (for instance, with its US engine, the Swedish Gripen can be marketed only in countries approved by Washington). Finally, Congress will not give the multi-year financial commitments that collaborative projects require.

To summarize more than 30 years of collaborative efforts, the Europeans have learned the disadvantages and gains involved, and are aware of the compromises that are often needed. They have often viewed collaboration as a terrible way to acquire equipment, only looking good when compared with any alternative. Insofar as the US seems aware of the compromises and cooperation needed to make collaboration work, it has been unwilling to accept them. The latest casualty in transatlantic efforts appears likely to be the US-German-Italian MEADS program, which France has already left; this is currently not receiving funding from Congress (*Defense News* 1998).

Significantly Europeans may now be moving away from traditional collaboration to procurement from multinational defence companies, which will be even more demanding in terms of the intergovernmental cooperation needed to underpin their activities. Europe is currently marked by joint ventures covering individual projects (such as Eurofighter GmbH), as well as more permanent joint ventures covering a series of projects in a particular field (e.g., Matra-BAe Dynamics and Thomson-Marconi Sonar). In addition, there are transnational strategic partnerships, including significant minority shareholding (such as BAe's 35 percent shareholding in Saab), and defence companies having fully owned subsidiaries in foreign states (with BAe's ownership of Heckler & Koch being a case in point). In December 1998, there were press reports of an imminent — but as it turned out very premature — merger of BAe and DaimlerChrysler Aerospace of Germany (*Sunday Times* 1998). In the event, and to the consternation of some in Europe, BAe moved to merge with General Electric instead.

Just as Europe appears to be moving away from traditional collaborative projects, the US seems to be considering them more seriously, not least because of the costs of some major systems, coupled with European reactions to pressures to buy. It appears that Washington has been anxious, even desperate, to recoup some of the R&D costs of the JSTARS system by inducing Europeans to acquire it. Unlike the previous parallel case of the AWAC system, where Europeans seem to have made a major contribution to American expenses, Europeans this time have not proved willing to buy an airborne ground surveillance system off-the-shelf from the US. Even if the UK does buy a system based on US technology, it will want some development work of its own. If Europeans become more reluctant to buy American complete systems virtually off the shelf, the US may feel a need to offer development work (i.e., collaboration) at an earlier stage than hitherto. The NATO ACCS system may finally advance as a transatlantic project, but transatlantic cooperation on ballistic missile defence will generate some powerful challenges.

EUROPEAN DEFENCE INDUSTRIAL RESTRUCTURING

At this point the argument should return to the earlier contention that transatlanticism, given existing industrial structures, will be a euphemism for American domination and that the most important and fundamental issue in transatlantic defence industrial relations concerns American attitudes and policies toward possible European defence industrial restructuring. This is a much more important matter than individual projects such as Tracer or even the UK role in the JSF.

No one should be misled by American complaints about the possibility of European defence trade protectionism (*Financial Times* 1998). For more than 40 years the US has been far more protectionist regarding its defence market than have European states. It is almost unthinkable that Europeans would turn their backs entirely on American defence equipment. Indeed the UK, which has been a strong proponent of industrial restructuring in Europe, has also shown a great readiness to buy from and even collaborate with the US. In complaining about lack of maximum access to European markets, American firms are seemingly aiming at full domination of the world market. In 1994, the US Arms Control and Disarmament Agency (ACDA) estimated world military expenditure at $840 billion, of which the US accounted for $288 billion (34 percent). Europe in its entirety represented a further $299 billion (36 percent) (US. ACDA 1996). It is perhaps not surprising that ambitious US defence businesses do not wish to see stronger European defence businesses.

Warnings about the emergence in Europe of monopoly suppliers in specific fields should also be treated with caution (*Financial Times* 1998). European monopolies are sometimes presented as damaging, because they would prevent the emergence of competing transatlantic teams in future collaborative projects. In some areas, European states will be able to sustain the operation of only one firm, not least because of the oligopolies created in the US. The bottom line will be whether American government and industry will want to see the emergence of strong defence industrial businesses based within Western Europe, or whether the US body politic will prefer the prospect of weaker, nationally based European companies. These companies could, of course, be fed with subcontracts from US defence industrial giants, just as the Canadian defence sector is today. Lockheed Martin likes to point to the 50 British companies with work on the C-130J.

It is easy to see how the US will be able to exercise pressure on European governments and companies. For instance, it could cut off orders to the US subsidiaries of foreign defence firms that have plants in the US (such as GEC and Rolls Royce) if those companies merge with other European firms. Further, it could manipulate access to US-classified information if it chooses to hinder European defence industrial restructuring. Washington could release a few nuggets of useful information to GEC and Rolls Royce, both of which have significant American investments, while demanding the information be restricted to UK eyes only. Such a stance would easily hinder the transformation of these firms into truly transnational entities. By working with BAe and Rolls Royce on the JSF, and by placing strict limits on how these companies use information derived from the project, Washington would be able to impede the establishment of European businesses in the aerospace area.

It is to be hoped, however, that Washington will take an enlightened view and encourage Western Europe to build defence businesses that can both compete and collaborate effectively with US firms. In this regard, the link between defence industrial competence and a general readiness in European countries to commit resources to defence needs to be highlighted.

NATO's newest strategic concept underlines the continuing importance of article 5 (NATO 1999). In addition, however, the US may want to see NATO as a means of organizing and mobilizing forces in support of international order in the environs of Europe, but also even beyond that continent. A NATO that incorporates US military and defence industrial dominance is not one that is likely to entice European voters to put resources into defence. Moreover, if European industry is weak, Europeans may just opt to buy its inferior products rather than further strengthen the American position by purchasing US goods. *De facto* protectionism in Europe could be a feature of a more fractured industrial position, and this would clearly imply a greater gap between the equipment levels of US and European forces.

CONCLUSION

The defence industrial situation is confronting Europeans and Americans alike with choices of massive importance. On one side of the Atlantic, governments and companies are moving, albeit slowly, toward a restructuring that would have enormous political implications. If national governments are to provide a customer base, a regulatory framework, and sponsorship arrangements for consolidated, integrated "European" defence businesses, they will have to increase drastically many aspects of their security cooperation. The Letter of Intent concerning "Measures to Facilitate the Restructuring of European Defence Industry," signed by six governments in July 1998, recognizes this.[3] On the other side of the water, America's government and companies will have to select policies to react to these European changes; sadly, there are signs that overall, the US will be reluctant to encourage the emergence of potentially rival defence firms in Europe. Finally, in the possible repertoire of American responses, the option of major US defence companies themselves seeking to buy businesses located in Europe cannot be overlooked. That possibility, and European reactions to such inward investment, remains beyond the purview of this chapter.

NOTES

1. This project is known in the UK as the Multi-Role Armoured Vehicle (MRAV).
2. Discussing this issue at the International Institute for Strategic Studies annual conference in September 1998, several participants pointed to the US Cold War attitude to technology transfer as a major obstacle to transatlantic defence collaboration.
3. The governments were France, Germany, Italy, Spain, Sweden, and the United Kingdom. The agreement pointed to cooperation needed regarding security of supply, export procedures, security of information, R&D, and the harmonization of military requirements.

REFERENCES

Defense News. 1998. "Pentagon Board to Make Last Ditch MEADS Choice." 19-25 October.

Financial Times. 1998. "Lockheed Chief Warns of Risks of 'Fortress Europe'." 30 October.

North Atlantic Treaty Organization (NATO). 1999. "The Alliance's Strategic Concept." Press Release NACS(99)65. 24 April.

Natural Audit Office. 1995. *Ministry of Defence: Eurofighter 2000*. London: HMSO. 11 August.

Sunday Times. 1998. "BAe Takes Off." 6 December.

United States. Arms Control and Disarmament Agency (ACDA). 1996. *World Military Expenditures and Arms Transfers 1995*. Washington: USGPO.

8

Transatlanticism versus Regional Consolidation: Lessons from the Canadian Experience?

David G. Haglund

INTRODUCTION

It might be asked whether Canada's defence industrial experience contains any "lessons" for the Western European allies as they ponder the future of their defence industries. This chapter approaches the question in two ways. First, it argues that to a significant degree it is impossible to discuss the Canadian defence industrial base as existing apart from the much larger American one; in a way, there *is* a North American defence industrial base, one moreover that exists in a dynamic tension with the emerging European defence industrial base (DIB), standing as it were as the other "pillar" of the transatlantic DIB — an architectural arrangement with both positive and negative implications, for Europe as well as for North America. Second, it makes sense to invoke the Canadian experience for heuristic purposes. There may be value for the United Kingdom and other Western European countries, either singly or collectively, in contemplating the manner in which, for better or worse, the Canadian DIB has evolved, namely as part of a tightly integrated, continental-scale defence market — yet at the same time a market with considerable transatlantic promise that remains to be realized (or, as the case may be, frustrated).

CANADA'S DEFENCE INDUSTRIAL BASE: ORIGINS AND IMPORTANCE

Canada's defence industrial base, like so many of its other socio-political institutions, was powerfully affected by the experience of World War II. From the country's founding in 1867 until 1939, Canadian military planning in general and defence-industrial policy in particular had been characterized, in one historian's colourful phrase, by "apoplectic mismanagement ... ill-preparation in peace punctuated by hectic and belated scrambles for munition preparation in war" (Haycock 1988, p. 71). That pattern would come to an end as a result of the global conflagration of 1939-45.

Beginning in 1940 and continuing to the present, the evolution of the Canadian defence industrial base has been heavily influenced by two developments. The first is closer cooperation with, and integration into, the American defence industry and market; the second is the shift away from the domestic production of major platforms toward a concentration on subsystems and components.

There are many ways of addressing the issue of the importance of Canada's defence industrial base. To start with, it must always be recalled that the reason states have defence industries is because they have goals the furtherance of which sometimes requires the possession and even use of military force. Thus it follows they have militaries, and since the latter need equipping, a defence industrial capability seems foreordained by the simple fact of states being desirous of surviving but also obliged to make their way in an "anarchic" international system, one that puts a premium on the principle of "self-help." That, at least, is how some theoreticians of international relations would account for the tendency of states to have defence industries (Waltz 1979).

But as everyone knows, not all states were "born equal," nor do they get about their affairs in precisely the same manner. Many states, conditioned *inter alia* by their relative standing in the international pecking order, come to see more promise and less danger in relaxing the autonomy imperative, allowing the processes of interdependence to bring to them things they seek, even if they are aware of the sacrifices and costs associated with interdependence. One such state is Canada, with a population and economy too small to permit self-sufficiency, and a territory too large to be defended entirely or even mainly by national means.

The geostrategic determinant, then, of the Canadian defence industrial base is ultimately the relationship with the United States. For, given power disparities on the North American continent, there is little Canada could do to defend itself in the event America had aggressive designs upon it, just as to the contrary there is much Canada does not have to do in the event America concludes that its own physical security depends upon its also protecting Canada from external aggression. The latter represents the current reality, and has ever since at least 1938, when President Franklin D. Roosevelt affirmed on Canadian soil, and in regard to the deteriorating situation in Europe, that the United States would guarantee the security of Canada against foreign invasion.

This is not to say that Canada's "America problem" means it has no need for a military, only that there is natural downward pressure on the size of the Canadian military as a result of Canada's geostrategic situation, even if that situation can at times seem a mixed blessing. This downward pressure applies *a fortiori* to the Canadian defence industrial base. As the country's ranking defence economist, Jack Treddenick, has written, an "ideal" defence industrial base must be able to accomplish two ends: it must provide for normal peacetime matériel needs of a country's armed forces; and it must be rapidly expansible in time of war or emergency, to meet and sustain increased demand. Canada's is far from an ideal defence industrial base in either sense, and as a consequence, the "Canadian option has been to import major weapons systems and to specialize defence production in a limited range of smaller systems, subsystems, and components, primarily for export. This specialization and trade in defence goods inevitably results in a mismatch between Canada's defence requirements and the structure of its defence industrial base" (Treddenick 1988, pp. 16-17).

A second point worth noting, derivative of the above, is that the macroeconomic impact of Canadian defence industries is limited, whether measured as a percentage of gross domestic product, of the total domestic workforce, or of the country's imports and exports (Wall 1991; Caron 1994). Data are not as readily available as they might be in countries with larger defence industries (and therefore more defence economists), but there seems little reason to dispute Treddenick's findings: "If economic significance means the amount of economic activity generated in the defence industries, then by comparison to total economic activity in Canada, the defence industrial base must be judged to be insignificant," accounting for "considerably less" than 1 percent of both GDP and total employment, for less than 1 percent of merchandise exports, and for about 2 percent of merchandise imports (Treddenick 1988, pp. 16-17; Canadian Defence Preparedness Association 1995/96; Canada 1997, pp. 69-70). Admittedly, within particular industry sectors (e.g., shipbuilding and repair) and geographic regions, the importance of defence production can be much greater.

A third, and final, general observation is warranted, and this is to reiterate that the Canadian defence industry is incapable of fulfilling the equipment needs of the Canadian Forces; this is so even though those Forces are getting smaller in number, shrinking from 85,700 uniformed personnel a decade ago to 60,000 by 1998-99. The Canadian defence industry has been neither structured nor tasked to fulfil those equipment needs since the late 1950s.

CHARACTERISTICS OF THE CANADIAN DIB

One particular characteristic of the Canadian defence industrial base is that it is composed primarily of small and medium-sized enterprises, with sales under $100 million a year. Foreign ownership of defence industries is also comparatively high — at more than 60 percent — in relation to the situation in other countries, and it is especially prevalent among the largest firms. This reflects, for the most part, the decision in the late 1950s to abandon domestic development of major systems; but it is also a consequence of subsequent policies governing industrial and regional benefits (IRBs), which require foreign companies competing for the Department of National Defence (DND) contracts to establish production facilities in the country. Finally, the Canadian defence industry is characterized by an extremely heavy dependence on exports in order to remain economically viable, with the largest percentage being sent to the United States (Edgar and Haglund 1995).

Within the defence industry, the major areas of strength are in aerospace, electronics, and communications, where there exists some capability for total systems-design integration. This capability, however, requires considerable technical and financial support, and this can be obtained or developed most easily by the subsidiaries of larger foreign companies. Significantly, defence production has been and remains geographically concentrated in Ontario and Quebec, particularly in the "golden triangle" of Toronto-Ottawa-Montreal.

A number of other basic strengths and weaknesses of the Canadian defence industrial base — opposite sides of the same coin, to a large extent — are commonly cited. Take the case of the integration of Canadian and American defence production. Geographic proximity can itself be an advantage, in part as the Pentagon seeks to maintain a reliable variety of "planned producers" of essential defence-related goods. But integration also causes a number of immediate and potential difficulties, not the least of which is the uncertain status of the bilateral defence economic sharing regime, given that without formal treaty status for the two sharing arrangements — the Defence Production Sharing Arrangement (DPSA) of 1959 and the Defence Development Sharing Arrangement (DDSA) of 1963 — the access of Canadian-based industries to the American market may remain subject to gradual erosion through the application of non-tariff and other barriers, as well as through the tightening of controls on technology export (*viz.*, the current dispute triggered by the US decision to cease exempting Canada from the State Department's International Traffic in Arms Regulations [ITAR]) (*Defence Policy Review* 1999).

It should not be thought that Canada's DIB is so integrated into the American one as to render the country's policymakers indifferent to opportunities for collaboration with other states, especially with other members of NATO. Quite the contrary: for reasons related both to economic and political/strategic advantage, Canada's idealized defence industrial base has come to be considered very much as a "transatlantic" one — arguably the only truly transatlantic DIB in the alliance. This is simply another way of remarking that the processes of globalization have advanced so much in the defence industrial realm that the effective Canadian "base" looks a lot like being coterminous with that of the Atlantic alliance.[1]

Or, at least it *would* so look if there could truly be said to *be* an alliance, or even transatlantic, DIB. That there has been an aspiration to foster such a defence base goes without saying; even and especially during the Cold War, appeals were frequently made (usually by American officials) to construct NATO's defence industrial base, so as to achieve needed rationalization in defence production as well as to limit the political friction occasioned by defence-industrial disputes between allies. But as the Cold War was drawing to an end a decade ago, it was possible — for a variety of reasons — to interpret trends on either side of the Atlantic as becoming more rather than less inward-oriented, and to conclude that the future of transatlantic armaments cooperation would be a Hobbesian one — nasty, brutish, and short. From the Canadian perspective, this was hardly a pleasant perspective. But was it an accurate assessment?

HOW FARES THE TRANSATLANTIC DIB TODAY?

It would be rash, and probably erroneous, to say it was an accurate assessment. By the same token, it would be equally rash to claim to know how the transatlantic DIB will develop in the future, or even *if* it will develop. This is because it is far from easy to obtain an accurate picture of today's transatlantic DIB, for seemingly straightforward "evidence" can lend itself to a variety of interpretations. Take the case of the merger announced in January 1999 between the British defence companies British Aerospace (BAe) and General Electric (GEC), which would have the former buying the latter's Marconi Electronic Systems in England as well as other defence holdings on the continent. Does this merger presage the construction, or the undoing, of a European defence industrial base? Is it good, or bad, for transatlantic defence relations?

To hear some in Washington discuss it, one would get the impression that it might lead to a closing of the European — or at least UK — market for American firms (because of the worry that British defence procurement would be contracted exclusively with this new "national champion"). Yet to hear the same merger discussed by officials on the continent, one would get the impression that the BAe-GEC deal has dealt a body blow to the quest for a more consolidated, and therefore competitive, European DIB.

That the aspiration for a more competitive European DIB continues to resonate among policy elites in the European Union (EU) may be taken for granted, all the more so since the Franco-British summit at Saint-Malo, France, in early December 1998, which seems to have breathed new life into the awaited European Security and Defence Identity (ESDI) by restating the need for the Europeans to develop new capabilities to take the lead in crisis-management tasks and humanitarian operations affecting their interests (Schake, Bloch-Lainé and Grant 1999; Schmidt 1999).

I will have a bit more to say about the ESDI later in this section. For the moment, let us take a glance at DIB developments in the United States, for part of the reason that Americans should have such difficulty reading the European DIB tea leaves stems from the general muddle surrounding the future of their own defence industrial base. There can be no question that the US has made much greater progress than Europe in "adjusting" its defence industrial base to the exigencies of post-Cold War defence spending. This has more to do with the efforts of the private sector than it does to any well-coordinated government strategy, for there seems to have been little *fundamental* change in government DIB policy from the Cold War era save for the policy line set down in the famous "last supper" in 1993, when Clinton administration officials informed industry executives that they should eliminate excess capacity by radical consolidation — in effect, they should "consolidate or evaporate" (Matthews 1999).

But the return of some portions of the American DIB to health was dependent upon more than consolidation. As Ann Markusen explains, the salvaging and restoration of the defence sector was a function of three different kinds of strategies among the large contractors. Consolidation, through mergers and acquisitions, represented one of these. The other two were downsizing and diversification (Markusen 1998). All three approaches have resulted in the flourishing of the American aerospace sector, which enjoyed record profits in 1998 of $7.4 billion, in part because so much of its business is now on the civilian side of the industry.

Significantly, most of this has been occurring not because of what the Department of Defense (DoD) was doing, but rather because of what it was *not* doing — namely discouraging mergers that in the past would have elicited anxiety among defence planners as well as other government officials. It seems, with the decision of the Justice Department to block Lockheed Martin's attempt to acquire Northrop Grumman in 1998, that the era of antitrust permissiveness has ended, at home at least. Does this, in turn, suggest that henceforth Washington will look less sanguinely at the consequences of "globalization" for the DIB? No one can say at this juncture. Though the Cold War might have ended, officials in Washington (especially at State and DoD) have continued to ponder how far America can allow itself to rely on "globalization" to secure for it needed defence equipment.

On the evidence to date, the answer would appear to be "not very far." What Lockheed Martin CEO Vance Coffman said at Munich in February 1998 remains true today: for there to be a genuine transatlantic DIB, the United States is going to have to demonstrate an "unprecedented willingness to be dependent upon others ... for some of the means to protect our security" (Coffman 1998). In many ways, absolutely nothing has changed in this respect from the close of the previous decade, when Secretary of Defense Frank Carlucci was touting intra-alliance armaments collaboration as a means of enhancing the common defence. If the NATO DIB was missing in action at the time of the alliance's fortieth anniversary, it remains missing today — at least at the level of *government* initiatives and programs. If anyone doubts such a claim, let them simply ponder this statistic: only one-twentieth of 1 percent of the Pentagon's budget for the year 2000 (i.e., some $142 million out of $268.2 billion) is allocated to international cooperative research, development, and testing programs, and even most of this trivial sum is gobbled up by just two initiatives: the US-Italian-German MEADS program (for Medium Extended Air Defence System), and the US-Israeli Arrow antimissile system (Opall-Rome 1999).

Defence industry, for its part, has been more active in forging — and in attempting to forge — links across the Atlantic, but whether it will succeed in bringing into being the mooted transatlantic DIB will have to depend on the willingness of governments to allow this to happen. Washington has yet to show such willingness, although the Pentagon has embarked on a series of studies aimed at trying to determine the implications of globalization for the country's security, with conclusions expected late in 1999 (Towell 1999).

And what of Europe? Again, the signals are mixed, as they are in the case of the United States. At some level there is a conviction that the process of endowing the ESDI with vitality must entail the defence industrial wherewithal to allow military missions to be mounted. This observation seems obvious to the point of being trite, and the only reason I introduce it is because it is far from clear, if defence considerations were all that were driving the debate over a European DIB *and* if the ESDI is going to be contained within the bosom of the Atlantic alliance, why kit could not be procured from the most economical source of supply, in the alliance or elsewhere. It may seem apparent to some in Europe (in particular, in France) that national or European "survival" depends on a relatively autonomous DIB, but it is less apparent from the Canadian perspective why this necessarily follows. At the risk of being provocative, while one could adduce a number of "threats" to Canadian sovereignty and security, it would be hard to muster a constituency for the preservation of an autonomous defence industrial base *as a sine qua non* for survival. Canadian policymakers worry much more about split-run editions of American magazines than they do about a Canadian DIB that is heavily integrated into the American one.

The European case for an autonomous DIB might better be made on economic grounds (jobs, after all, are at stake, and why should the public's tax pounds and Euros go into the coffers of foreign defence manufacturers?). Even better would be to make the case on a political-strategic basis, namely that a Europe with greater capability in defence *and* defence production is a Europe more able (and presumably willing) to share the burden of a common defence with the United States. This is in many ways a good argument, and the Europeans are wise to express their DIB initiatives in burden-sharing language. Hence the claim made by Lt. Gen. Jean Fournet, a high-ranking French procurement official, who awaits the coming of a European Armament Agency that, far from constituting a "Fortress Europe," actually implies just the opposite: the strengthening of America's European partners so as to make them more capable of furthering common Western interests (Fournet 1999).

Where the burden-sharing logic would fray, however, is if the inefficiencies introduced by intra-European collaboration began to *detract* from, not enhance, Europe's ability to shoulder its share of the load. Claude Serfati reminds us of the all-too common tendency of collaborative efforts undertaken in defiance of market logic to add to costs, and increase the time needed to take an idea from the drafting board to the airstrip, in citing the whimsical formulation of J. F. Delpech, namely that the costs of production increase by the square root of the number of partners (n), while the delays increase by the cube root of n (Serfati 1996).

For the moment, Europeans are arguing that consolidation accompanied by privatization will mean that collaboration adds value, and does not take it away. Once European industry becomes sufficiently robust, it is held, then genuine and "balanced" partnerships can be crafted on a transatlantic basis.

CONCLUSIONS

Two conclusions emerge from the analysis in this chapter. First is that the transatlantic DIB remains to be constructed; perhaps if NATO has a sixtieth anniversary someone will be prompted to remark on the amazing progress made by the allies in building the alliance's defence industrial base. But as between the fortieth and fiftieth birthdays, the best that could be said is that scant progress was registered. Moreover, if the pace is going to quicken in the coming decade, it will almost certainly result from industry rather than government initiatives, and will likely require British industry to play a central part in the process of transatlantic consolidation (for reasons that are too numerous to state here) (Black 1999). For their part, governments will have to establish permissive conditions; this applies to Washington even more than it does to European capitals.

The second conclusion returns us directly to this chapter's subtitle: are there lessons for Western Europe from the Canadian experience? In contemplating the current shape and future prospects of the Canadian defence industrial base, it might be well for the observer to ponder Samuel Johnson's remark about a dog's walking on its hind legs: "It is not done well, but you are surprised to find it done at all." To the surprise of many, Canada retains a defence industrial base, one that may have problems, but also has formidable strengths in certain niche markets. Perhaps what has occurred in Canada will point the way to the future for European arms industries, surviving if at all only as parts of a globalized system of production, arrayed along a transatlantic axis.

Caution is in order, however, regarding the attempt to generalize for Europe from the Canadian experience, and this for one very good reason: defence industries are not ordinary industries. They exist, presumably, because there is a need for defence. I have argued in this chapter that due to a geostrategic reality perhaps unique to North America, there are upper limits to what Canada arguably "needs" to spend in the quest to ensure its physical safety. Indeed, the real issue is not whether there is a ceiling, but rather where to locate the floor, of defence spending. There is, after all, special geostrategic meaning for Canada, living as it does on "a continent apart" (Fox 1985).

For the Western Europeans, the situation may be different. Quite apart from the postulated requirement to build a European defence industrial base for the purpose of building "Europe," there is the question — which must remain open — of the degree to which the Western Europeans can afford to entrust their physical security to far-off lands, no matter how favourably disposed those lands may be to come to Europe's defence. There are actually three components to this question.

First, structural-realist theoreticians of international politics like to argue that balancing behaviour is an "iron law" of international relations, and for some of them this means that states (or aggregations of states) will always have to balance against more powerful states, for their own security. Thus, Kenneth Waltz has little difficulty foreseeing a day, in the not-too-distant future, when Western Europe will be obliged to balance against the power of the United States (Waltz 1993, p. 50). Waltz is not alone, but even if one rejects the lugubrious forecasts of the structural realists, there still remain two "benign" reasons for Western Europe to maintain its defence industrial capability.

These are actually two sides of the same coin, each having to do with the commitment of future North Americans to European security. It may develop that NATO becomes so "transformed," especially through its enlargement, as to constitute more of a cooperative-security than a collective-defence entity. In that case, while a "security community" might continue to characterize transatlantic relations, there would be no assumption that North American military forces would automatically be deployed to safeguard European members of the alliance. The other side of the commitment coin assumes that NATO remains a credible collective-defence organization, but that increasingly the problems of European security take the form of crisis-intervention in so-called "out of area" contingencies, say in the Balkans or elsewhere on the periphery of Western Europe. (Although the experience with Kosovo might dampen the impulse to undertake such interventions in future.)

In either of these latter cases, it might be hypothesized that if the Europeans were increasingly going to be bearing the burden of defending their own part of the world, they will have to be assured of having the equipment needed for the task. It is far from obvious, at least to this writer, that they could not purchase what they might need from the United States, if it came to that. As well, there is always the prospect of Combined Joint Task Forces resolving their equipment dilemmas for them.

This leads us back, then, to the "lugubrious" scenario of the structural realists. In the end, perhaps Canada's geostrategic situation is not all that different from that of the European allies. Unless one can foresee a time when Europe and the United States become strategic rivals, then it becomes more and more difficult to make the case that Europe's *political* future — or at least its "survival" — depends in any meaningful way upon its having a defence industrial base that is relatively autonomous from the North American one.

NOTE

1. It needs to be pointed out that even to suggest there is a NATO defence industrial base can be controversial; at the very least, it seems such a base today reflects more of a policy aspiration on the part of some observers rather than a political reality. For that aspiration, see Moodie and Fischmann 1989; and Coffman 1998.

REFERENCES

Black, C. 1999. "Britain's Atlantic Option and America's Stake," *National Interest*, 55(Spring):15-24.

Canada. 1997. *Making Sense Out of Dollars: 1997-1998 Edition*. Ottawa: Department of National Defence.

Canadian Defence Preparedness Association. 1995/96. "The Budget Challenge," *National Network News*, 8(Winter):15-17.

Caron, S. 1994. "The Economic Impact of Canadian Defence Expenditures," Report No. 23. Kingston: Centre for Studies in Defence Resources Management.

Coffman, V.D. 1998. "The Future of Transatlantic Industrial Partnerships," paper presented to the 34th Munich Conference on Security Policy.

Defence Policy Review. 1999. "ITAR — An Interview with Eric Newsom Conducted by Dale Grant." 5, 17 May, p. 2.

Edgar, A.D. and D.G. Haglund. 1995. *The Canadian Defence Industry in the New Global Environment*. Montreal and Kingston: McGill-Queen's University Press.

Fournet, J. 1999. "European-U.S. Balance," *Defense News*, 22 February, p. 33.

Fox, W.T.R. 1985. *A Continent Apart: The United States and Canada in World Politics*. Toronto: University of Toronto Press.

Haglund, D.G., ed. 1988. *Canada's Defence Industrial Base: The Political Economy of Preparedness and Procurement*. Kingston: Ronald P. Frye.

―――― 1989. *The Defence Industrial Base and the West*. London: Routledge.

Haycock, R.G. 1988. "Policy, Patronage, and Production: Canada's Private Munitions Industry in Peacetime, 1867-1939," in *Canada's Defence Industrial Base*, ed. Haglund.

Inbar, E. and B. Zilberfarb, eds. 1998. *The Politics and Economics of Defence Industries*. London: Frank Cass.

Markusen, A. 1998. "The Post-Cold War American Defence Industry: Options, Policies and Probable Outcomes," in *The Politics and Economics of Defence Industries*, ed. Inbar and Zilberfarb.

Matthews, W. 1999. "U.S. Mergers Drive Boeing, Lockheed to Diversify," *Defense News*, 22 February, p. 14.

Moodie, M.L. and B.C. Fischmann. 1989. "Alliance Armaments Cooperation: Toward a NATO Industrial Base," in *The Defence Industrial Base and the West*, ed. Haglund.

Opall-Rome, B. 1999. "Pentagon Pares Cooperative Program Spending," *Defense News*, 15 February, p. 6.

Schake, K., A. Bloch-Lainé and C. Grant. 1999. "Building a European Defence Capability," *Survival*, 41(1):20.

Schmidt, P. 1999. "Neuorientierung in der Europäischen Sicherheitspolitik? Britische und Britisch-Französische Initiativen." SWP - AP 3088. Ebenhausen: Stiftung Wissenschaft und Politik.

Serfati, C. 1996. *Les industries européennes d'armement, de la coopération à l'intégration*. Paris: La Documentation française.

Towell, P. 1999. "Does Security Suffer as Pentagon Shops in the Global Marketplace?" *Congressional Quarterly*, 13(February):401-04.

Treddenick, J.M. 1988. "The Economic Significance of the Canadian Defence Industrial Base," in *Canada's Defence Industrial Base*, ed. Haglund.

Wall, P.H. 1991. "The Economic Impact of Canadian Defence Expenditures, FY 1989/90 Update," Report, No. 21. Kingston: Centre for Studies in Defence Resources Management.

Waltz, K.N. 1979. *Theory of International Politics*. Reading, MA: Addison-Wesley.

―――― 1993. "The Emerging Structure of International Politics," *International Security*, 18(2):44-79.

PART THREE

DEFENCE INDUSTRIAL POLICY DILEMMAS

9

Who Defends the Defence Industry?

Paul D. Manson

INTRODUCTION

At the outbreak of war in 1939, Canada had no defence industrial base to speak of, yet within months the country was producing huge quantities of war material: Canada's industrial contribution to the ultimate victory was phenomenal, especially given that its population at the time was only 11 million. Today, some 60 years later, things have changed so radically that it might be said that the "lessons of the past" hold little if any meaning.

This is not to deny that certain similarities exist between the two eras. In the 1930s, Canada's navy, army, and air force had been allowed to run down to minuscule levels, the victims of a depression economy and of a society that was blind to the emerging threats from Nazi Germany and Imperial Japan. In our own time, Canada's regular forces have been reduced from a postwar high of 125,000 to the current figure of less than half that. Defence budget cuts in the past decade have amounted to about 30 percent, largely the result of a widespread public belief that the risk of Canada's involvement in a major war has become virtually zero with the end of the Cold War.

In these circumstances, not surprisingly, the Canadian defence industry has declined rapidly, to the point where by no means does it constitute a "defence industrial base" in the classical sense. Nor is Canada's situation all that unique, at least among Western countries. Even the United States and the United Kingdom have to cope with some fundamental problems facing their defence industries in a time of quantum change.

Nevertheless, for Canada these changes are so profound, and their interactions so complex, that it is far from easy, even in theoretical terms, to define the role of and the need for an indigenous defence industry. The very concept of a defence industrial base as an element of national security strategy comes into question. One might even ask — at least in the Canadian context — if there is any point, in the era of globalization, in defining a national policy that promotes the maintenance of a national defence industry specifically structured to support the armed forces.

SHOULD (OR DOES) CANADA HAVE A DEFENCE INDUSTRIAL BASE?

Any attempt to impose a modicum of analytical order upon this complex issue must begin with an examination of the very powerful forces that exert their influence on the defence industry, and which have such an important bearing on the future of companies that are in the business. In this respect, the logical starting place is an examination of the strategic environment, which is a window upon what the military prefers to call the "threat assessment." Without some understanding of the possible forms the military threat might take, and the sort(s) of conflict that might result, there can be no sense of direction concerning the defence industry.

The "problem" in 1999 (of course, it is also a blessing) is that there is no manifest military threat facing the West today, at least of the kind that might lead to a large-scale war in the short- to medium-term future. The Cold War, although it took place in the scary atmosphere of potential nuclear confrontation, was much easier for planners in the sense that they had a measurable threat in the Soviet Union and its allies. In other words, they knew something about the enemy's military capabilities, and could plan accordingly. This enabled them, with some precision, to design effective deterrent forces, and these in turn defined the defence industry that was called upon to equip and support those forces.

Today, by contrast, governments are denied the luxury of a well-defined threat, and are forced to resort to a generalized defence strategy, and to the multi-purpose armed forces that go with it. The last Canadian defence policy statement, the 1994 *Defence White Paper*, put it this way:

> The Government has concluded that the maintenance of multi-purpose, combat capable forces is in the national interest. It is only through the maintenance of such forces that Canada will be able to retain the necessary degree of flexibility and freedom of action when it comes to the defence of its interests and the projection of its values abroad (Canada 1994, p. 13).

In a later section, the document's drafters went on to state that such multi-purpose, combat-capable forces required the "support of a technologically sophisticated industrial base to be effective."

In the years since those noble policy statements were written, the Canadian government has had great difficulty in following through. If anything, the multi-purpose combat capability of the Canadian Forces has deteriorated, and a cohererent industrial base can scarcely be said to exist in this country today. This inability to convert policy aspiration into reality is not uncommon among NATO governments. It is simply a reflection of the bewildering complex of factors touching on the defence industry, including, especially, the role of technology.

There is a powerful tendency to resort to the astounding advances in technology that have occurred over the past several decades as a panacea. The digital revolution in particular offers all sorts of "force multipliers," as justification for reductions in the scale of standing forces. Space platforms, sophisticated sensors, instant communications, precision-guided munitions, battlefield computers, and countless other new products and techniques have dramatically changed the nature of warfare. This "revolution in military affairs" has altered and in many ways strengthened the bond that exists between the armed forces of a country and the industry that supports them.

But the new military technology is so diverse, and its required infrastructure so imposing, that a country of Canada's limited industrial means and scope cannot expect to be autonomous across the whole spectrum of technology. Canada stopped producing main battle tanks in 1945. It gave up trying to design and produce its own fighter aircraft with the demise of the Avro Arrow in 1959. Although the Canadian defence industry did create a fleet of outstanding frigates for the navy in recent years, the absence of follow-on orders has resulted in a breakup of the design and production teams, and it seems likely that from now on Canada will have to procure its capital warships abroad. The country has not produced a large military transport aircraft since the Yukon in the 1960s, and even that was a derivative of the Bristol Britannia.

And so it goes. A combination of factors, mostly economic, has driven Canada's defence industry into a relatively small set of companies turning out highly specialized products such as flight simulators, small aircraft engines, wheeled armoured personnel carriers, communications systems, and other defence electronics. The industry seems to do these things very well, but the fact remains that Canada, increasingly, must purchase its military equipment abroad.

The net result is that it does not have a defence industrial base that by itself could sustain the armed forces in time of war, in periods of extended crisis, or even in peacetime. Fortunately, much of the Canadian Forces' equipment comes from such staunch allies as the US and the UK. However, it cannot realistically be expected that Canada's priority would be very high in an emergency and at a time when its allies would likely be struggling to meet their own domestic surge requirements.

CURRENT CHALLENGES: GLOBALIZATION AND DEFENCE BUDGETS

For years, NATO has tried to introduce a degree of rationalization into the alliance's defence procurement process. One such activity was an attempt to distribute certain defence product lines as specialties among the various national industries. For example, Country A would specialize in medium-range air-to-air missiles, Country B in submarine sonar, etc. Not surprisingly this rationalization did not work, because of vested national interests and economic realities

In a sense, the internationalization of the world's high technology industry has achieved much the same result as NATO's rationalization program set out to attain. Global companies, by definition, distribute their work geographically on a rational economic basis, in response to international market forces rather than to political edict. Giant companies such as Boeing, Lockheed Martin, British Aerospace, and Aérospatiale are large enough to produce the major weapons systems whose development costs are frequently in the hundreds of millions of dollars. In these undertakings cross-border alliances and joint ventures are the order of the day. Multinational development programs are commonplace. Standardization and interoperability become second nature throughout the industry.

Thus, internationalization and its logical extension, globalization, have rendered obsolete the very idea of an autonomous, national defence industrial base, at least for the second- and third-tier members of the alliance, Canada included. Even the United States, which in the Cold War years staunchly resisted any sort of reliance on industries other than its own, today seeks international partners in the development of major systems, such as the Joint Strike Fighter.

But globalization on its own cannot account for the demise of an autonomous defence industrial base in Canada. The Canadian defence establishment has in recent years witnessed a dramatic decline in its share of tax dollars, in the face of competing demands for better social programs and the paydown of the country's enormous national debt. Although Canadians seem to want well-equipped and well-trained armed forces, it is a quaintly Canadian paradox that they are not prepared to pay the price for these. With the end of the Cold War, and with their geographical isolation from the world's trouble spots and the comfortable presence of Uncle Sam south of the border, Canadians have been quite happy, by and large, to watch their defence budget shrink from an already low level of $12 billion a year to $9 billion during the 1990s.

As for the defence industry, many Canadians seem to share the governing Liberal Party's notion that it should "convert" its skills and means of production away from military products and into peaceful pursuits. It should be noted, however, that the "swords into plowshares" phenomenon, as an instrument of government policy, has not distinguished itself with an abundance of successful examples, to paraphrase Norm Augustine, chairman of Lockheed Martin.

On the other hand, and rather ironically, market forces *have* been managing to effect what governments cannot: the move into civilian product lines. The Department of National Defence's capital procurement budget, expressed as a percentage of the total defence budget, has fallen from around 24 percent to 16 percent in the past decade, and this at a time when the total budget itself has declined by 30 percent. This constitutes dreadful news for the defence industry, because the capital budget is the lifeblood of the industry. Many companies have been forced to cut the size of their operations substantially, while others have disappeared altogether or have been caught up in mergers and acquisitions. Even companies that export a high percentage of their output of defence goods and services have felt the pinch, because of similar cutbacks in customer countries, and as a consequence of the growing intensity of global competition in the defence marketplace.

THE DEFENCE INDUSTRIAL FUTURE: WHAT SCOPE FOR POLICY INNOVATION?

Clearly, these are difficult times for the defence industry in Canada, and the story is much the same in other allied countries. One has to wonder how far current trends will go. More importantly, are there policy decisions that could or should be made to ensure that national armed forces have the kind of industrial support they need as they move into a very uncertain future?

The prevailing notion in Canada remains that the country is very unlikely to find itself in a hot war of major proportions, and that the kind of rapid military build-up experienced in 1914, 1940, and 1950 is not going to be repeated. Any lower intensity war involving Canada, such as the Gulf War or the Kosovo intervention, would be a "come-as-you-are" enterprise. It is interesting to note, however, that in the build-up to the Gulf War, the Canadian defence industry was called upon to make some very quick "lash-up" improvements to old naval ships before they could be of any use in theatre, and it is interesting to recall that the United Kingdom had a similar experience with some of its weapons systems at the outbreak of the Falklands War. In both cases, industry came through very quickly and very well.

The important lesson here is that repair and overhaul (R&O) capability constitutes an essential element of the domestic defence industry in the era of high-tech weapons systems, and states allow it to wither at their peril. Fortunately, R&O capability is relatively easy to safeguard, since governments usually have it within their power to establish the requisite skills and industrial capacity. For example, when Canada negotiates the purchase of a major new weapons system, such as fighter aircraft or submarines, the deal carries enough leverage to allow the government to insist upon the transfer of sufficient technology to the home industry for the establishment of a solid R&O base here.

Another policy device that successive Canadian governments have attempted to use is the idea of creating "centres of excellence" within the domestic defence industry. According to this model, procurement policy is designed to encourage the development of a world-class capability for a given technology within a specified Canadian company — not unlike the NATO rationalization program discussed above, save that it applies at the national level. The concept has enjoyed limited success at best, for the simple reason that it smacks of government favouritism, and that it stultifies competition and interferes with natural market forces. There are in fact centres of excellence in the Canadian defence industry today, but these are the product of global competitiveness, not of government intervention.

A more sensitive question is the issue of subsidization, which can take many forms. For years, Ottawa extended numerous grants and loans to defence firms under the so-called Defence Industry Productivity Program, or DIPP. The emphasis was on R&D, and loans were supposed to be paid back from royalties if and when the resulting product became profitable.

Several years ago the DIPP was replaced by a much more modest program called Technology Partnerships Canada, in which the defence industry is only one of several industrial sectors receiving benefits. Recently, there has been much criticism of this program and its predecessor, which are referred to disparagingly as "corporate handouts," even though the industry itself declares them to be vital to the development of global competitiveness and to the support of the armed forces. In any case, the amount of financial support for the defence industry that comes from such programs in Canada today is more or less inconsequential. R&D spending by the industry continues to be alarmingly low, in spite of an R&D tax-credit environment that is very generous.

One recent development worth mentioning is the trend toward commercial management of what were hitherto military activities, such as the operation of large military bases and shipyards. Both the US and UK have been doing this for some time, with considerable success. Canada has recently turned over the management of its basic flying training and helicopter training programs to Bombardier, and a similar venture is underway for the new NATO flying training program in Western Canada, again under contract to Bombardier.

There can be little doubt about the efficiencies generated by this concept of "Alternative Services Delivery" by industry, but there is a certain degree of uneasiness on the part of military staffs about the possible weakening of the country's warfighting capability and loss of core military skills.

CONCLUSIONS

Several conclusions can be drawn regarding the quest for rational solutions to the problems of the defence industry. First, the global strategic and economic environments have changed so drastically in the past decade that the classical concept of an autonomous national defence industrial base is no longer valid, at least for countries like Canada.

Second, it probably does not much matter. It is inconceivable that Canada could find itself fighting alone against some as-yet undefined enemy, without recourse to the large international defence industrial base that exists in the West today, and with which Canada has such close ties.

Third, artificial government measures to structure the defence industry, at least at the macro level, probably will not work, whether these be attempts to establish specific new technologies within favoured companies, or indeed to force companies out of the defence business by imposing conversion policies upon them. Better by far to allow the competitive market to determine who does what and who survives. On the other hand, at the micro level, there is much that can be done by government and by the industry itself to make the latter more effective. There is a great need in Canada to improve and streamline the capital equipment procurement process, which has become ludicrously cumbersome. Nor is Canada alone in this regard.

The Department of National Defence set out in the mid-1980s to acquire a fleet of maritime helicopters to replace the aging Sea Kings. Today, some dozen years later, after several false starts, there is still no contract; in fact, no formal competition is even under way, and it looks as though the 35-year-old Sea Kings will have to be kept in the air for at least another six years. Although part of this particular problem is political, it seems likely that a better procurement process would have resulted in new helicopters being now in service.

One last conclusion can be offered. Ultimately, companies are in business to make a profit, and only competitiveness can ensure profitability in the long term. One thing is certain: if there is a genuine need in a given country for a specific industrial capability in support of the military, we can be sure that some enterprising company is going to provide it, and make a profit doing so. Contrary to previous experience, however, that company may very well be in another country.

Thus, the principal general observation is that the defence industrial base itself has been internationalized, if not globalized, within the community of democratic countries, as part of the free market economy. In other words, the defence of the defence industry is ultimately the responsibility of companies, not of governments.

REFERENCE

Canada. 1994. *1994 Defence White Paper*. Ottawa: Department of National Defence.

10

Beyond the Dollar Crisis: Defence Strategy and Procurement in Canada

James Fergusson

INTRODUCTION

It is widely recognized that defence ranks extremely low on the political agenda in Canada, and this extends from the political élite to the public at large. It is also evident that the willingness of government to provide adequate capital equipment for defence requirements is similarly low. As a result, capital expenditures or procurement not only face the problem of obtaining support from government, but also become significantly affected by, or liable to, a variety of political, economic, and social considerations largely divorced from an abstract idealized vision of procurement stemming from relatively strict strategic-military logic or dictates.

Canada, of course, is not unique; every country faces a variety of non-strategic factors that affect the level and nature of capital spending. In the case of Canada, however, these non-strategic factors are, arguably, much more pronounced. How much more so, and why, are the questions that frame this chapter's examination of the relationship between strategy and procurement in Canada. It is my contention that the problems confronting that relationship are hardly limited to the lack of funding, as important as that might be.

THE CANADIAN EXCEPTION

At the root of the dilemma lies the simple reality that Canada faces no direct immediate threat to its national security. Since its inception, or at least since the formal recognition that the United States was no longer a direct military threat to its territorial integrity, Canada's national-security interests have been linked to regions far beyond its borders, especially to Europe. Even during the Cold War, in which Canada found itself sandwiched geostrategically between the two super-power adversaries, the tendency to look to Europe remained predominant. To be sure, Canada did participate in continental defence with the US, primarily through the North American Aerospace Defence Command (NORAD), but this commit-ment, even for the country's air force, was somewhat circumscribed by the con-cerns of domestic politics, with the result being that it was, more often than not, portrayed as being linked to the broader commitment to European security. This is not to say that the linkage generated more in the way of resources to meet commitments, for it did not (Byers 1986).

With the ending of the Cold War, the problem of matching resources to com-mitments has not disappeared. The 1994 *Defence White Paper* emphasizes capability-based planning as a key determinant of Canadian commitments. The strategic requirement is the maintenance of combat-capable forces able to con-tribute to allied, coalition, and UN actions as necessary. Rhetoric aside, it is pain-fully evident that the Canadian Forces (CF) remain limited in respect of what missions they can actually undertake. Moreover, it is highly likely that future capability will be less than current capability. The result may be a gradual drift toward the preferred outcome of "Canada 21," namely a military limited to under-taking traditional-style peacekeeping and little else (*Canada 21* 1994).

To date, the Department of National Defence (DND) and the CF have been fighting a rearguard action. They have attempted to rationalize and prioritize capital acquisitions in order to meet the strategic requirement. However, recent and planned future capital acquisitions indicate that tensions among competing interests re-main unresolved, as we shall see below.

THE ENDURING "COMMITMENT-CAPABILITY GAP"

Clausewitz's famous adage — war is a continuation of politics by other means — may be often stated, but it is nevertheless frequently ignored. Instead, strategy in many cases seems to be grounded within a strict military rather than political logic. The political factors that determine decisions to go to war, and the objec-tives to be sought through war, can too often be pushed into the background. The result is that "strategy" becomes strictly a military consideration, useful for de-fining the capabilities required for victory.

In this section I regard strategy as something a bit different, namely the process through which ends are related to means in a "rational" (i.e., cost-effective) sense. The ends are, and must always remain, political ones. Ends and strategy, thus, constitute the road map for procurement. In their absence, procurement has no rational meaning.

The basic parameters of Canadian defence policy — the "road map" — can be found in the 1994 white paper (Canada 1994). As is the case with most government policy documents, one finds therein generality and ambiguity; nevertheless, a relatively specific set of procurement or capital spending priorities can be identified, and this notwithstanding budget cuts implemented in the years subsequent to the document's release. This implies that capital spending will continue to lag (Canada. House of Commons 1998).[1]

It would be relatively easy to dismiss the Canadian situation with the breezy recognition that the funds are not available to meet capital priorities and requirements, and therefore there is little else to say: the combat capabilities of the CF will simply deteriorate through "rust-out" and obsolescence in the relatively near future, and that will be the end of it. But this would be too simplistic. What is needed is to examine critically capital priorities within the context of Canadian ends and strategic considerations, rather than to concentrate exclusively upon budgetary factors.

So what does the white paper identify as the strategy? It states that Canada "continues to have a vital interest in doing its part to ensure global security" (Canada 1994, p. 3). This commitment to global security underpins the recognition that the "most appropriate response is a flexible, realistic and affordable defence policy, one that provides the means to apply military force when Canadians consider it necessary to uphold essential Canadian values and vital security interests, at home and abroad" (ibid., p. 8). The relationship between forces required (the "means") and the contribution to global security (the "ends") is twofold, involving the country's international security commitments (e.g., NATO, the UN) and the strategic requirement to maintain multi-purpose, combat-capable forces. This articulation reflects the principle of internationalism, which has been the hallmark of Canadian strategic thought since World War II.

There have, it is true, been attempts to adopt a more nationalistic strategic posture: witness the 1971 defence white paper (Canada. Parliament 1971). But, even in this case, the nationalist posture was soon abandoned, to be followed by a resumption of internationalism and by significant reinvestment in Canadian military capabilities as largely determined by the NATO commitment. For a time, attention shifted to capabilities, the argument being that Canada's commitments could not be met unless significant new resources were provided above and beyond those implied by the reinvestment that occurred during the 1970s. Even though the 1987 white paper, entitled *Challenge and Commitment*, pledged to close the gap by providing more resources to the CF (Canada 1987), the domestic fiscal situation, coupled with the Cold War's waning, would lead to the "death" of this ambitious document in 1989.

Subsequently, the manner in which the "commitment-capability gap" was conceived began to change. Henceforth, the emphasis would be placed on the capabilities rather than the commitments, or so it was thought. This adoption of a capabilities-based strategy was predicated upon the new post-Cold War strategic environment, and assumed an ongoing fiscal retrenchment. According to many observers, Canada now had the opportunity to make choices about its commitments. While to some this signalled the end of the country's alliance involvement, for the majority it meant something different, namely a greater freedom to choose, and this in turn indicated that decisions about participation in military coalitions would often become dependent upon the existence of capabilities. But old habits died hard, and in this case the tug of voluntarism made the alleged primacy of capabilities seem a bit hollow. This is demonstrated not only by the aborted mission to Zaire in late 1996 but also by Ottawa's support for the development of an effective UN "rapid reaction capability," and its commitment to the Danish-sponsored UN Standby Rapid Reaction Brigade — both of which speak to a deeply ingrained "internationalist" strategic outlook (Fergusson and Levesque 1996/97).

This is to suggest neither that such a strategy is inherently wrong for Canada, nor that capability-based planning is a myth. For a country such as Canada commitment-based strategy would seem to be politically indispensable, for it constitutes the primary means of attaining some influence in the domain of international security realm. Commitments become the price of entry for a range of political objectives. This does not suggest capabilities are irrelevant; but it does suggest that the "commitment-capability gap" may be an eternal aspect of Canadian strategic debate.

BALANCING ENDS AND MEANS IN THE LATE 1990s

During the Cold War, it was believed (correctly) that maintaining forces for the dominant strategic scenario would also provide the capability for other missions, including aid of the civil power and peacekeeping. However, the post-1989 strategic environment introduced a new logic, and with it a fundamentally revised view of military engagement, stressing low-intensity interventions of a relatively long duration. At the same time, it was also recognized that in these probable engagements, potential adversaries would be relatively well-equipped, even if not necessarily organized or trained as a traditional conventional army. As a result, planning became more rather than less complicated.

The result was that it also became more difficult to understand what being "combat-capable" actually entailed. To resolve this dilemma, planners made more frequent resort to "scenarios" (Canada. Auditor General 1998a, pp. 3-22). The 1999 Defence Planning Guidance identifies no fewer than 11 such scenarios as currently under development. Of these, two would rank near or at the top of the intensity scale: scenario 9 concerning peace-support operations, and 11 relating to collective defence. The former implies a Gulf War-style operation, and the latter an attack upon a NATO ally (Canada. Department of National Defence 1999, pp. 3A1-3A2).

Significantly, it appears that "combat-capable" does not refer to forces-in-being able to prosecute war on a high-intensity battlefield. Rather, scenarios 9 and 11 are best construed as mid-level operations. Furthermore, assuming that scenario 9 is grounded on the Gulf War, it would appear that the distinction between high- and mid-level conflicts is twofold. First, it likely excludes the use of weapons of mass destruction. Second, it is also likely to include all arms/armoured warfare against a relatively well-equipped adversary, but not one of the first or second tier of military capacity (referring, respectively, to the US and most of its NATO allies). With this in mind, it may be possible to assess whether recent, current, and projected future capital acquisitions provide the capabilities to meet Canada's expressed strategic preference, of contributing to international peace and stability.

CONTRADICTIONS OF PROCURING MID-LEVEL COMBAT-CAPABLE FORCES

Fundamental to such an assessment is the recognition of the paramountcy of "interoperability" with allies and potential coalition partners. "Interoperability" needs to be understood in the context of NATO's dominant powers, the US and the major European allies. If Canada is interoperability with these, it follows that it can be interoperable with others.

It is important to ascertain the relationship between recent, current, and planned "major capital projects" (MCPs) and mid-level combat-capable forces. The white paper states that Canada requires forces able to "fight alongside the best, and against the best" (Canada 1994, p. 14). Against the "best" needs to be qualified so as to refer to the "best" at mid-level conflict. With this in mind, the white paper further states that it would be "misguided to invest in very specific forces and capabilities, whether at the high end of the scale (aircraft designed for anti-tank warfare, for example) or at the lower end (forces limited to minimal-risk peace-keeping)" (ibid.).

There can be little doubt that the procurement strategy of the Canadian Forces eschews the purchase of highly specialized equipment. For example, the Canadian air force has gone from possessing multiple air platforms performing single missions to single platforms performing multiple missions. The CF-18 is now the single fighter in the service, with its capability for multiple roles enhanced by the acquisition of precision-guided munitions (PGMs), whose effectiveness was demonstrated in the air war against Serbia. The twin helicopter fleet for army support has been replaced by the Griffon. Finally, planners had intended to replace the single-mission maritime and search and rescue (SAR) helicopter by one platform, the EH-101.[2]

In many ways, the multi-role platforms are now available due to modular technology advances that also enable significant life-extensions. Moreover, such platforms do reduce costs in logistics, maintenance, and training — a vital requirement in the current fiscal environment. Finally, such platforms are consistent both with ensuring mid-level combat-capable forces and with providing a general capability. However, underlying these acquisitions, is the unspoken tension between general purpose forces and specialized or "niche" forces.

Canadian strategy had long called for the maintenance of general purpose forces, even though the specific reference to these was dropped in the 1994 white paper in favour of multi-purpose, combat-capable forces. However, despite the earlier stated preference for such forces, the reality was different: specialized or "niche" forces represented reality for the CF, and have done so for the past several decades, rhetoric to the contrary notwithstanding.

Since World War II, the pace of Canada's progression toward specialized, niche forces has picked up. During the Cold War, the navy carved out a special role in anti-submarine warfare, surrendering its power-projection capability. The air force abandoned its strategic bomber capability in favour of air defence in North America and interdiction/ground attack in Europe. In many ways, it was only in the army that general forces remained an aspiration, albeit not without difficulties concerning main battle tanks (MBTs). Today, the niche seems to reign supreme, with Canada's navy playing a sanctions-enforcement role, its air force a combat air-patrol one, and its army an armoured reconnaissance/light mechanized infantry one (symbolized by recent purchases of the light armoured vehicle [LAV] in different variants).

For all that, the drift to specialization has been, and remains, anathema to many within DND and the CF. There has in fact been no conscious commitment to take the path of specialization; it has rather been a necessity decreed by lack of resources. Indeed, recent acquisition decisions might even be read as confirming the preference for general capability; in this regard one can cite the decision to upgrade the Leopard 1 MBT with thermal sighting. Even though the tank will continue to be relatively obsolete on the modern battlefield, this upgrade will extend its life and combat utility for mid-level conflicts. Another useful example, apropos the theme of this volume, is the recent purchase of Upholder submarines from the United Kingdom: the service case for submarines spoke directly to the strategic requirements for balanced naval forces and the ability to be operative in all three maritime dimensions — above, on, and below the surface (Maritime Command 1994).

In many ways, the emergence of specialized niche forces, coupled with the reluctance to recognize this reality, is a product of the internationalist commitment strategy. Ironically, the desire to maintain general forces to the maximum extent possible may, in fact, undermine the very goal of ensuring that Canada *can* make a meaningful contribution, as a result of a confusion between "core" and combat capabilities.

Official government documents use core capability and combat-capable interchangeably. For example, the Defence Planning Guidance 1999 states: "The Government has stated that multi-purpose combat-capable forces need not, and should not, cover the full range of possible military force capabilities. The CF will thus only maintain core capabilities suited to a wide range of defence roles. In this context, modernization efforts, guided by force planning scenarios, will focus on those operational capabilities that clearly support approved roles and tasks so that essential capabilities are not lost due to rust-out or obsolescence" (Canada. Department of National Defence 1999, p. 2-1).

There appears to be an assumption that core and combat capabilities are synonymous. However, in respect of the MBT decision, it is obvious that the upgrade does not provide the army with the capability to undertake combat operations even at the mid-level. In the case of the Gulf War, the unspoken basis for scenario 9, many observers suggested that the Canadian army did not participate because the Leopard 1 was inferior to Iraqi armour capabilities, and thus a liability. This was not the only, and perhaps not even the most important, reason for the decision not to send ground troops. Nonetheless, even an upgraded Leopard will likely have little combat utility. Instead, the upgrade testifies to a desire to ensure that capability is not completely lost. A similar argument has been made in regard to submarines over the last decade, and likely will be made again in future capital acquisitions.[3]

The Leopard upgrade to the contrary notwithstanding, it is highly unlikely that Canada will ever acquire another MBT. Instead, plans are afoot to acquire an armoured combat vehicle (ACV) after the completion of the three phases of the current APC Coyote program. The ACV is apparently intended as a direct fire-support vehicle for the APC, and will likely possess a 105-mm gun on a redesigned LAV chassis. While the ACV will certainly be combat-capable, it is not a tank. Once (or if) acquired, its deployment as part of Canada's brigade commitment would reinforce the country's niche role.

Though the tension between core and immediate combat capabilities has not yet surfaced completely, it is likely to do so in the future, even if the capital budget rises significantly. As the CF has drifted to specialized forces, so it has lost core capabilities. There has, to be sure, been resistance to the drift, stemming in part from departmental and service "culture" (Bland 1995). While "objective" strategic requirements cannot be ignored in understanding procurement decisions, neither can the influence of cultural images derived from the organization itself be disregarded. Thus, for the army, an MBT requirement, regardless of opportunity costs, fits an organizational image drawn from past experiences. By their nature, armies require the full range of combat capabilities that include armour, infantry, and artillery. Similarly, the self-image of a modern combat-capable navy includes a submarine requirement, even though the Canadian navy did not acquire submarines until the 1960s.

Moreover, the submarine acquisition is inconsistent with the scenario-based capability discussed above. There is scant strategic logic to be mustered in support of the maintenance of a submarine capability for mid-level combat scenarios. In fact, the submarine case is largely a Cold War anachronism, derived from assumptions about anti-submarine warfare and sea lines of communication. Moreover, the case for submarines as a cost-effective means to attain national-sovereignty ends, even under favourable purchase conditions and reduced outlays when compared to the existing Oberons, ignores opportunity costs in a period of fiscal constraint.

This is not to suggest that the Upholder decision lacks political, or even strategic, value; on the contrary, its value really lies in cooperation with allies, especially the US and UK. Facing potential conventional diesel submarine threats, Canada now possesses a valuable asset for American and British Navy nuclear submarine training that will enhance, and protect, the wide range of benefits accrued from close cooperation. It may not be interoperability per se, but it does reflect the commitment- and coalition-based strategy of Canada, in which the country's requirements cannot be divorced from allied requirements. This perspective, however, is a politically sensitive one in Canada, given its long-standing concerns about independence and its relationship with the US. Above all else, political sensitivity also raises the final strategic dimension in understanding procurement in Canada — the fact that economic interests can be much more salient for political élites than are the political-military interests.

THE POLITICAL-DEFENCE INDUSTRIAL CONSTRAINT

The strategy-procurement nexus does not involve only military and civilian professionals. It is also a relationship defined by outside political-economic forces, and these constrain choices further. At the core of this constraint is the obvious recognition that capital spending in defence, even at relatively low Canadian levels, represents a substantial amount of investment by Ottawa into the industrial sector. Capital projects are regularly the largest single purchases of government. As a result, capital-spending decisions are not couched in strictly military or defence terms; they are also economic decisions, with all the associated political connotations.

Two key factors have structured the evolution of Canada's domestic defence industrial base. The first was the recognition that the Canadian market was insufficient to maintain a fully integrated, independent defence industrial capacity. The second was the obtaining of privileged access to the American defence market through the negotiation of the Defence Production Sharing Arrangement (DPSA), through which Canadian firms were, with certain restrictions, to be treated as American firms in Department of Defense (DoD) procurement competitions.

The result was the evolution of a defence industrial base largely dependent upon, and structured to serve, the American market as second-tier subsystem and component suppliers to DoD and American defence prime contractors. This is not to suggest, however, that the smaller Canadian market was unimportant to Canadian firms, or that the Canadian government played no role in shaping the industrial base. On the contrary, Canadian contracts, as well as such support mechanisms as the lapsed Defence Industrial Productivity Program (DIPP), were important in providing avenues for the development of Canadian products that would be leveraged into export opportunities, primarily to the US.[4]

More importantly, Ottawa also established an offset program under the label of Industrial and Regional Benefits (IRBs) to ensure that defence dollars would be spent inside Canada. IRBs were to be the vehicle for developing a Canadian industry that could partially serve Canadian defence requirements, and be internationally competitive. In addition, they were to entice foreign firms, especially American ones, to establish relationships with Canadian firms, and also set up their own production facilities in Canada. Finally, the regional component of the program would provide a means to distribute limited defence dollars across the country.

IRBs, or "offsets," have experienced a variety of iterations (Fergusson 1996). They have structured Canada's defence industry, as well as its procurement policy, in a manner that constrains and in many circumstances dictates acquisition decisions. They have done so by fostering an industrial dependency in which defence requirements become structured to meet industrial needs. For example, Ottawa purchased the Griffon helicopter from Bell Helicopters in Montreal, even though helicopter production had previously been rationalized by Bell, with military production being centralized in the United States. The Griffon, as a result, emerged as a militarized version of a commercial helicopter. More importantly, as pointed out in the recent Auditor General's report, the Griffon cannot meet the army's military lift requirements (Canada. Auditor General 1998*b*). It has further been argued that the Griffon constitutes a military liability on a mid-level battlefield, because of its lack of armour and self-defence weapons. While the aforementioned logic of rationalizing Canada's helicopter fleet from three platforms to a single one should not be ignored, the economic logic of supporting a major Canadian industry in a politically important area at a sensitive time should also not be ignored.[5]

Two other aspects of the Griffon decision are important. First, any procurement decision will have implications for future decisions on associated equipment. In the case of the Griffon, its purchase was followed closely by the decision to procure the French Giat light 105-mm howitzer. With the inability of the Griffon to lift the existing 105-mm howitzer, the acquisition of an artillery piece that it could transport became essential. Second, it appears that the large capital investment into Quebec had to be matched, for political reasons, by an investment elsewhere; in this case the result was a decision to procure the LAV from GM Diesel in Ontario. The LAV and follow-on purchases also indicate the extent to which military requirements become captured by industrial demands. One should not dismiss the military capabilities of the LAV. Nonetheless, the existence of this major production facility in Canada was an important independent factor in the procurement decision, with significant implications for the future.

For instance, the debate over the relative value of "wheeled" versus "tracked" armoured vehicles may have been settled in favour of the former on economic and political grounds. There is logic in procuring a single family of armoured vehicles, given today's budgetary realities; significant costs savings are generated through replacing single-role platforms with multi-role ones, especially in training and maintenance. That said, a single family of armoured vehicles based on the LAV design does limit the roles and missions of the Canadian army. The LAV is not an armoured infantry fighting vehicle, as is the M-2 Bradley; nor will the ACV based on the LAV design with a 105-mm gun become an MBT. Even in situations of mid-level combat, the army will have limited battlefield capability. This is an outcome that is determined, to some important degree, by industrial rather than by military considerations, whether decisionmakers admit it or not.

FUTURE PROCUREMENT CHOICES

If past practices are any guide, the future ACV purchase (if one occurs) can be said already to have been settled in favour of a LAV variant produced by GM Diesel. This reflects the "rules of the game" in Canadian procurement. For the capital-starved Canadian Forces, one of those rules is to demonstrate that there will be Canadian economic, and thus political, benefits accruing to its capital and procurement choices (Fergusson 1998). This, in turn, implies that if there is a Canadian production facility, then operational requirements will likely be shaped to meet the existing industrial capability. Should there not be any Canadian production or prime facility, then foreign bidders for contracts will have to promise economic and political benefits.

In this context, it is still possible for defence considerations and preferences to prevail, as seems to have been the case with the Cormorant (EH-101) purchase. However, even in such instances in which military requirements do come out on top, there will be implications for future procurement. For example, the original decision to replace the Sea King ship-borne and Labrador SAR helicopters with the EH-101 came under attack as a "rigged" exercise. The statement of requirement (SOR) was said by critics to have been written to fit the EH-101. Similarly, the decision pursuant to the cancellation of the EH-101 to purchase the Cormorant version for SAR alone was held by losing bidders to be unfair.

Politically, this raises questions about the forthcoming ship-borne replacement. Depending upon the SOR, it is possible that political reasons alone will be invoked so that an image of fair competition can be ensured, even though the military logic of the past two decades (i.e., of rationalizing capital acquisitions to obtain multi-role platforms) remains unaltered. In other words, under the current and future fiscal environment facing DND, the logical choice would seem foreordained: the Cormorant. But making that choice will both reveal and reflect the "structured false competition" appertaining to Canadian acquisitions. By the same token, *failing* to make that choice is also problematical, for it would result from political pressures that are far removed from the reality facing the Canadian Forces. If procurement officials ever faced a "damned if you do, damned if you don't" situation, this would seem to be it.

In effect, the capital acquisition or procurement process in Canada may well be defined as in the paragraph above, as "structured false competition." When there exists a prime-contractor production facility in Canada, military requirements will be defined in terms of that facility. When such a facility does not exist, foreign competitors will need to structure their "Canadian content" creatively enough to allow the Canadian military some freedom to choose on the basis of military requirements — within, it needs to be said, the envelope of funds available from Treasury Board and with due regard to input from such other government departments as Foreign Affairs and International Trade, Industry Canada, and Public Works.

Ultimately, and this should come as no surprise, the combat capabilities of the CF will in part continue to be a resultant of the existing nature of Canada's defence industrial base. In future, it may turn out that there will be a weakening in the established linkage between military and industrial capabilities, for government policy seems increasingly to be emphasizing a reliance upon market forces, rather than political ones, in the procurement process. This seems more a recognition of necessity than proof of genuine conviction, for governments are interventionist by definition, especially in the defence marketplace, where they are, after all, the sole consumers.

Even should Ottawa come to embrace the logic of the commercial marketplace, there will always remain plenty of room for exceptions, which "will be assessed on a case-by-case basis for items of a unique or strategic nature where intervention is warranted" (Canada. Department of National Defence 1998). This caveat reflects a tension already evident in the 1994 *Defence White Paper*, in which "spending smarter" and "off-the-shelf" purchasing coincided with the expressed desire to ensure industrial benefits and meet broader economic goals (Fergusson 1995).

While it is always possible to believe that future "exceptions" will be driven by strict military requirements, it is much more likely that they will result from economic and political necessity. Recently, for example, the minister of national defence sought to ensure that a Canadian producer would not be excluded from competition for a new light utility military truck, even though this producer's truck does not meet two established criteria, namely that it already be in production and that it be field-tested (Pugliese 1998).

CONCLUSIONS

This chapter has identified a series of factors, transcending fiscal restraints, that subtend the relationship between strategy and procurement in Canada. In part, these factors and the problems they create can be chalked up to the lack of importance of defence, and defence-related issues, in Canada. In the absence of any direct military threat to it, the defence of Canada has tended to become a non-issue of late. Partly, this is a reflection of domestic economic concerns, as well as of political questions associated with the preservation of national unity.

It is true that defence used to matter to Canadians for reasons related to "nation-building" as well as to protection from external aggression. Of late, however, defence has been unable to muster the same degree of political support, and this shows up in the unwillingess of Canadians to commit scarce resources to it. Not surprisingly, the strategic value of commitments diminishes, in lockstep with the diminution in the willingness to make the capital investments required to honour commitments.

How long can the underinvestment in defence be expected to continue? One senses that a breaking point is near to being reached, for a shrinking capital budget will increasingly force "hard choices" upon those responsible for planning the future of the CF. Today the country spends on capital equipment the meagre annual sum of $1.45 billion. There is little likelihood of any increase in this amount. As a result, decisions will have to be made regarding which projects to support, delay, or cancel. Above and beyond existing capital commitments, there loom on the procurement horizon the ship-borne helicopter, the ACV, the CF-18 and Aurora modernizations, and the Joint Space Project. The cost of the CF-18 alone is estimated at $1.2 billion, to be spread out over eight years. The Aurora is said to require a further $1 billion.

Even with a steady capital budget and imaginative financing arrangements it is difficult to see where the money will be found. Delays and "stretch-outs" are always options, but other replacement and modernization demands will emerge, and technology does not stand still. The challenge is magnified by the demands of interoperability; for Canada does not fight alone, and unless the CF are interoperable, they may not be able to fight at all.

NOTES

1. Even though the federal budget has moved into surplus, it is unlikely that defence will benefit, given such other priorities as debt-reduction, tax cuts, and increased spending in health. Moreover, the capital budget itself may be increasingly vulnerable as a result of demands to redirect defence funds to other needs, such as "quality-of-life" issues. In the budget of February 1999, defence spending increased by $175 million, but this amount was insufficient to offset the estimated $700 million costs of quality-of-life, to say nothing of the impact of defence inflation.
2. The EH-101 was cancelled by the Liberals immediately upon taking office in 1993, despite the costs (estimated at nearly $600 million) of the cancellation. A version of the EH-101, the Cormorant, has been chosen to replace the SAR Labrador, and the maritime version is now reportedly to begin the competition process.
3. Another example is the mid-life CF-18 modernization, as well as long-term questions about its replacement. The CF-18 is seen as vital for combat support operations, especially in the absence of a ground attack helicopter capability. However, unless the CF-18 demonstrates its usefulness, obtaining funds for modernization is likely to be problematical and the core capability argument is likely to become prominent, along with allied interoperability. With regard to a future replacement, DND has invested a small amount of funds to obtain observer status on the Joint Strike Fighter (JSF) program. This investment enables the department to obtain knowledge about potential technologies useful for CF-18 modernization, and leaves the door open to the JSF as a future replacement.
4. The DIPP has been replaced by the Technology Partnerships Canada (TPC) program, which has been expanded beyond defence into other sectors. Most recently, the TPC was struck down by the World Trade Organization (WTO) as an unfair trade subsidy. The particular case concerned TPC funds to Bombardier in Quebec.
5. The logic of rationalizing platforms also extended into the naval sphere with the aborted decision to procure the EH-101 to replace both the ship-borne Sea King and search-and-rescue Labradors. In 1998 Ottawa announced a purchase of the Cormorant,

the EH-101 by another name, to replace the Labradors, with the Sea King replacement still pending. Interestingly, no one considered the procurement of a single platform for army, navy, and SAR roles. The ideal candidate would have been the Sikorsky Black Hawk (the Sea Hawk being the naval variant). Of course, Sikorsky does not have a major production facility in Canada.

REFERENCES

Bland, D. 1995. *Chiefs of Defence: Government and the Unified Command of the Canadian Armed Forces*. Toronto: Brown.

Byers, R.B. 1986. *Canadian Security and Defence: The Legacy and the Challenges*, Adelphi Paper No. 214. London: International Institute for Strategic Studies.

Canada. 1971. *Defence in the '70s: White Paper on Defence*. Ottawa: Department of National Defence.

———— 1987. *Challenge and Commitment: A Defence Policy for Canada*. Ottawa: Department of National Defence.

———— 1994. *1994 Defence White Paper*. Ottawa: Department of National Defence.

Canada. Auditor General. 1998a. "National Defence: Equipping and Modernizing the Canadian Forces," in *Report of the Auditor General of Canada to the House of Commons*. Ottawa: Supply and Services Canada.

———— 1998b. "National Defence: Buying Major Capital Equipment," in *Report of the Auditor General of Canada to the House of Commons*. Ottawa: Supply and Services Canada.

Canada. Department of National Defence. 1999. *Defence Planning Guidance 1999*. Ottawa: Supply and Services Canada.

———— 1998. Director General International and Industry Programs. *Defence Industrial Policy and International Relations with Industry*. Ottawa: Department of National Defence.

Canada. House of Commons. 1998. Standing Committee on National Defence and Veterans Affairs. *Moving Forward: A Strategic Plan for Quality of Life Improvements in the Canadian Forces*. Ottawa: Supply and Services Canada.

Canada 21: Canada and Common Security in the Twenty-First Century. 1994. Toronto: University of Toronto Centre for International Studies.

Fergusson, J. 1995. "The Missing Dimension of the White Paper: A Defence-Industrial Strategy," *Canadian Defence Quarterly*, 24(4):6-10.

———— 1996. "In Search of a Strategy: The Evolution of Canadian Industrial and Regional Benefits Policy," in *The Economics of Offsets: Defence Procurement and Counter-Trade*, ed. S. Martin. Netherlands: Harwood.

———— 1998. "Getting It Right: Canada and the American National Missile Defence," *Canadian Defence Quarterly* 27(4):20-24.

Fergusson, J. and B. Levesque. 1996/97. "The Best Laid Plans: Canada's Proposal for a United Nations Rapid Reaction Capability," *International Journal*, 52(1):118-41.

Maritime Command. 1994. *The Naval Vision: Charting the Course for Canada's Maritime Forces into the 21st Century*. Ottawa: Department of National Defence.

Pugliese, D. 1998. "Critics Assail Eggleton Vehicle Program Move," *Defense News*, 7-13 December.

11

The Politics, Economics and Ethics of Arms Exports

Philip Gummett

INTRODUCTION: WHY DO STATES BUILD AND SELL ARMS?

Following Krause (1992), we can suggest that states have three main motivations for supporting military industries:

- Pursuit of victory or survival in war, meaning national security benefits, such as independence of arms supply; quid pro quos for security-related deals; a contribution to collective security; and being able to match equipment supplies to specific national requirements.

- Pursuit of power and identity, meaning influence over élites in recipient states in pursuit of the supplier's foreign policy objectives; symbols of security commitments and national status; the creation or maintenance of a balance of power or regional presence; and access to strategic resources.

- Pursuit of wealth, meaning a range of economic benefits including foreign exchange and balance of trade; maintenance of employment/infrastructure; recovery of R&D costs; and the use of military production as a driver of economic development.

The first of these is a traditional military or defence-oriented motive. The second is more political in outlook, and the third relates more to the economic realm.

Since the end of the Cold War, several European governments, and the US and Canada, have had more difficulty articulating clearly why their military industries deserve public support, at least on the present scale. In each of Krause's three categories, the claims made for the industries seem to have weakened. Below

I consider these in turn, referring in particular to statements made in the UK in the summer of 1998, in the Strategic Defence Review (SDR) (UK. MOD 1998b).

PURSUIT OF VICTORY OR SURVIVAL IN WAR

Wars have become more common around the periphery of Europe, but a general war engaging the entire military resources of the transatlantic alliance no longer seems credible. Indeed, the Strategic Defence Review acknowledged that

> The world does not live in the shadow of World War. There is no longer a direct threat to Western Europe or the United Kingdom as we used to know it, and we face no significant military threat to any of our Overseas Territories (UK. MOD 1998b, para. 23).

To say this is not to deny arguments for maintaining capabilities against the longer term, or to minimize the new vulnerabilities to which advanced societies are exposed, such as information warfare, or biological weapons (UK. MOD 1998b, paras. 29-34). Nor is it to overlook the numerous interventions in which UK forces are today engaged.

Nevertheless, the ensuing equipment requirements, and arguments over security of supply, are somewhat different from those of the Cold War. The argument for buying British is also much diminished, to the extent indeed that, even in defence circles, some thought is known to have been given to meeting Britain's need for heavy airlift capability by buying Russian aircraft.

PURSUIT OF POWER AND IDENTITY

European nations are currently too weak, or too constrained, to take much interest in global power games, and even the possible development of a "Fourth Pillar" of the European Union (EU), concerned with security matters, would not easily change this reality. But the UK continues to highly value cooperation with the US, and sees a clear need, therefore, to keep the so-called technology gap sufficiently narrow in enough areas to enable that cooperation to have a solid basis. Ideally, the UK would even be ahead in a few.

In addition, Britain's vital interests, as the SDR argued, are not confined to Europe. The economy is founded on international trade, with exports forming a higher proportion of gross domestic product (GDP) than for the US, Japan, Germany, or France, and with a higher proportion of income being invested abroad than for any other major economy. Hence, Britain's economic interests and history give it other international responsibilities, not least because ten million of its citizens live and work abroad. "Our national security and prosperity thus depend on promoting international stability, freedom and economic development." Moreover, as a permanent (veto-wielding) member of the UN Security Council, and "as a country both willing and able to play a leading role internationally," Britain has a "responsibility to act as a force for good in the world" (UK. MOD 1998*b*, para. 21). This argument, in other words, continues to carry weight in the UK, alongside the contrary proposition concerning Europe more generally, referred to just above.

PURSUIT OF WEALTH

The economic benefits from military production are not as straightforward as is sometimes claimed, either in terms of direct benefits or, given today's relative scales of investment in civil and military research, in terms of technological spin-off. There are several arguments to lay out here.

First, consider what might be termed the "orthodox defence" of arms exports:

> Defence exports remain very important to the British economy and to British defence equipment manufacturers who ... secured contracts worth about £5 billion in 1995. This gave the United Kingdom its second highest market share ever, and maintains our position as the world's second largest exporter of defence equipment. Indeed, in no other major industrial sector is the United Kingdom achieving some 20% of the world export market. The British defence industry as a whole supports nearly 400,000 jobs, and between a third and a half of the industry's output, in monetary terms, is for export. Exports also help maintain Britain's essential technology base and reduce the unit cost of equipment purchased for use by our own forces (UK. MOD 1996, para. 445).

Note the references to the scale of these sales, to their significance in underpinning an internationally competitive industrial base, and to their importance to the national technology base. Similar points were made in the Strategic Defence Review:

> Defence export orders have reached over £5 billion per annum. They are beneficial not just to Britain's economy, but directly to the MOD. Savings to MOD through reduced fixed overhead charges resulting from exports amount to some £350M per year. In addition, the MOD also benefits through receipts from Commercial Exploitation Levy payments for the use of products whose development it has funded. These receipts have averaged some £50M per year over the last five years (UK. MOD 1998*b*, Essays, pp. 10-30).

An interesting twist to this argument comes from Davina Miller, in a book entitled *Export or Die: Britain's Defence Trade with Iran and Iraq.* The title is taken from the evidence of David Mellor, MP, former minister of state for foreign and commonwealth affairs, to the Scott Inquiry into the exports of defence equipment and dual-use goods to Iraq. In examining why this belief is held so firmly, Miller contends that it is not sufficient to try to explain British arms sales simply in terms of the familiar argument about the desirability of maintaining the defence industrial base (and the associated desire to defray development and production costs over the longer production run that exports permit). She argues, correctly, that the economics of arms exports (including the question of the level of support given by government agencies — see below) lack transparency, so making it difficult to establish precisely what benefit does accrue. Moreover, and regardless of defence industrial base concerns, ministers, as she shows, and as we saw above, have supported arms exports on the broad ground that it has been an area of relative export strength against a background of generally weak performance by the UK manufacturing sector.

However, she also suggests that full explanation of the political and economic significance of British arms sales must also take into account not only wider foreign policy interests, among which lies a general concern to maintain influence over importing countries, but also a specific desire not to rock the boat for potential *civil* exports of *greater economic value*. As she demonstrates, if trade no longer follows the flag, it may still follow the gun. At the very least, denial of guns may damage wider trade prospects.

We should also draw attention to the standard counter to the orthodox defence of arms exports, as expressed in the following quotation:

> In a period of declining national defence markets, the pressures for companies to export arms overseas are increasing. In fact, the Defence Export Services Organisation (DESO) has stated that the UK companies should be seeking to double their exports to 50% of their output. Ethical objections to arms exports are over-ruled on the grounds that exports are essential to maintain jobs in the defence sector.... [Yet] in a crude calculation ... each defence-export job directly costs the government at the very least £7,250 in subsidies (this figure represents around half the average wage of a defence contractor employee) (Oxford Research Group 1998).

In other words, the income earned from defence exports needs to be set against substantial public costs incurred in generating that income.

The figure for what in the quotation is called "subsidy" is computed by taking the costs, as disclosed in parliamentary questions and other official sources, of DESO, trade fairs support, defence attachés, use of the Armed Services for demonstrations, claims paid by the Export Credits Guarantees Department (ECGD) and other ECGD costs, aid transfers, and an element of MOD procurement expenditure, principally for research and development (R&D), that the researchers attribute to defence exports.

Three comments can immediately be added. First, this author's own recalculation of the Oxford Research Group's figures suggests an arithmetical error (£760m/

145,000 jobs = £5,241/job, not £7,250). Even so, the revised figure remains substantial. Second, it must be recognized that some of the costs identified would have arisen anyway, regardless of their application to this particular purpose. An example would be the costs attached to use of the Armed Forces who, if not engaged in demonstrating defence equipment, would no doubt have had other useful employment. Third, the largest item in the calculation is that for R&D said to be related to exports. The researchers estimate this at £470 million, but it is difficult to be clear on what basis this estimate could reliably be made. To put the point another way, it is difficult to say what savings in R&D might be made if no exports were to be sought.

However, to make these points is not to deny the essential argument that defence exports do benefit from support of the kinds indicated. MOD itself regards the work of DESO, and of other modes of support of arms exports, as being cost-effective (see again the second quotation, above, in this subsection). But to say this is nevertheless to acknowledge the investment that MOD itself is here making. It is also true, to take only the R&D argument, that without the substantial investment made by MOD, over many years, in advancing defence technology within its own research establishments and through development contracts placed with firms, those firms would not enjoy the strength that is currently theirs in the export market. The difficulty (impossibility, perhaps) lies in putting a cash value on that benefit.[1]

The third element of the "orthodox defence," cited above, relates to the contribution of defence exports to the national technology base. In this respect, it is worth adding that pre-election statements from the then Labour opposition referred to the sharp reduction that was taking place in defence industry employment, and advocated establishment of a Defence Diversification Agency (DDA) designed to provide information on long-term procurement plans and on best practices in diversification, assist in identifying new markets and areas for R&D, including improving technological spin-off from defence research, advise on the targeting of European Union KONVER grants, and coordinate renewal in highly defence-dependent areas affected by base closure or industrial retrenchment (Labour Party 1995).[2] We also saw in the years prior to the May 1997 election significant action by the Defence Evaluation and Research Agency (DERA) to establish Dual-Use Technology Centres, at which to develop cooperation between DERA itself, together with companies and universities, of technologies with both defence and civil value.

The main point to make in this regard, however, is that in key fields of advanced technology, the balance of investment has been changing in the last decade or so, such that today the level of civil investment in R&D in some fields vastly exceeds that of military investment (Gummett and Reppy 1988; Gummett and Stein 1997). Indeed, the SDR itself recognizes this development (UK. MOD 1998*b*, 3-1, para.7), although it does not itself quite draw the conclusion that this observation undercuts arguments about the spin-off benefits that can be expected these days from the defence sector. In short, while MOD investment in technology remains economically important, arguments that defence *exports* help maintain the national technology base ring considerably less true today than they used to do.

THE POLICYMAKING PROCESS

Licences for defence exports from the UK are issued by the Department of Trade and Industry (DTI). DTI considers applications on a case-by-case basis, and seeks advice from MOD and the Foreign and Commonwealth Office (FCO). Contributions may be made by a multiplicity of actors inside and outside those departments, including DESO, the intelligence agencies, the ECGD and the Treasury, not to mention non-governmental bodies such as defence companies and assorted pressure groups.

The decision-making process takes into account a set of criteria that include UN embargoes, specific government policy positions in respect of individual countries, and international treaties or codes to which the UK has subscribed. In the past, these included the COCOM agreement. Today, they include the Nuclear Non-Proliferation Treaty, the Missile Technology Control Regime, the Chemical Weapons Convention, and EU codes governing arms sales (see below) and exports of dual-use technologies. Of particular significance, especially in the context of "ethical foreign policy," is the question of whether defence equipment might be used for internal repression, or for international aggression.

In terms of how the policy process works in practice, decision making over specific export deals is, suggests Miller, precisely that — *specific* (and in saying this, she echoes the language routinely used within government of "case-by-case" consideration of licence applications). That is to say, and unsurprisingly, there is no algorithm underlying British arms export policy, but only a general framework of guidelines and procedures within which particular cases are *negotiated* by the various interested parties. It is worth noting that this activity takes place under considerable pressure: during the 1980s, typically 80-90,000 export licence applications were processed per year, implying about seven applications per staff day. There is, therefore, inevitably a great deal of management by exception (Miller 1996, pp. 37-38). Given the balance of forces within the process, there is also clearly a presumption in favour of awarding the licence.

Nevertheless, Miller rejects bureaucratic politics and organizational process models as a basis for explaining these decisions. Rather, she argues, policy is driven from the centre, with the prime minister and foreign secretary as the most important actors. The elaborate machinery for assessing applications for export licences then becomes an interdepartmental forum for testing competing arguments, but within the framework of a clear pre-existing policy preference, and with the interests held in common by the participants outweighing those over which they differ. Here, in fact, is one of the points of disagreement between her book and the Scott report, with its rather more amorphous picture of the decision-making process.

This point has significance for thinking through the implications of any new steer to the policy framework that might emerge from an "ethical foreign policy" (see below). It implies that the scope for change depends heavily on the political will that is expressed at the heart of government.

If Miller is right, there may be more prospect of the UK system delivering a change than did the US system under Jimmy Carter. Spear has described how presidential candidate Carter believed that traffic in arms threatened world peace. He promised, and in 1977 introduced, a tough new arms transfer restraint policy, designed to reduce US arms exports progressively year by year. Yet barely two years later, the new policy had for the most part been abandoned. Spear tells a salutary tale of how the best intentioned plans came unstuck in the large and complex US bureaucracy. She shows how apparently technical criteria (such as that the US would not be the first to supply weapons that introduced a higher level of technology into a region) turned out to be political in practice; and how the competing goals of top political appointees, *and* the routine decision making of lower level officials, both undermined the policy. The devil of the failure lay in the detail (Spear 1995). If Miller is right in her analysis, however, the conclusion may be that the UK governmental system is more steerable from the top than that of the US on a matter of this kind. What kind of steer, therefore, can be expected?

ETHICAL ARGUMENTS

The orthodox economic defence of arms exports has an ethical counterpart:

> The Government believes that the responsible transfer of defence equipment is consistent with Article 51 of the United Nations Charter, which recognises the inherent right of all states to self-defence. That right cannot be exercised unless states also have the right to acquire the means by which to defend themselves. The transfer of conventional weapons, when conducted in a responsible manner, can enhance the ability of states to meet their legitimate defence and security requirements; contribute to the deterrence of aggression; encourage negotiation for the peaceful resolution of conflict; and enable states to join effectively in collective measures decided by the United Nations for the purposes of maintaining or restoring peace and security (UK. MOD 1996, para. 448).

To this classical argument can be added further arguments in terms of the government's responsibility for protecting the livelihoods of defence industry workers and their families. However, from mid-1997, a new dimension was added to the British politics of arms exports, with the statement from the new foreign secretary that:

> Britain will refuse to supply the equipment and weapons with which regimes deny the demands of their peoples for human rights. Last month, I announced a review of Government criteria for the licensing of weapons for export. That review will give effect to Labour's policy commitment that we will not supply equipment or weapons that might be used for internal repression.... [It] will result in changes to the present policy governing the licensing of riot control vehicles, small arms and other equipment for sale to the security forces of certain regimes (Robin Cook, MP, foreign secretary, 17 July 1997).

Initially, however, there were no obvious signs of significant changes in actual decisions. In its 1998 Yearbook, the Stockholm International Peace Research Institute (SIPRI) noted in respect of this policy shift that, at the same time, the government had committed itself to a "strong and successful defence industry" and to maintaining "its leading position." With the exception of some export licence refusals to Indonesia, regarding equipment for internal security, by early 1998 this new policy did not, said SIPRI, "seem to have changed much in the usual practice of British arms exports" (SIPRI 1998, p. 297).

Consistently with its new position, however, Britain used its presidency of the EU in the first half of 1998 to help steer to a conclusion the lengthy discussions on the development of an EU Arms Trade Code of Practice (*Financial Times*, 26 May 1998). Under this Code, when making decisions about arms export licences, EU member states agree to take into account human rights in the country of final destination, and the internal security situation in that country. They also agree to have regard to the preservation of regional peace, security, and stability; to the behaviour of the buyer country with regard to the international community, not least as regards terrorism; to the existence of any risk that the equipment would be diverted within the buyer country or re-exported under undesirable conditions; and to the compatibility of the proposed exports with the technical and economic capacity of the recipient country. If they decide not to issue a licence in a particular case, they inform the governments of the other member states accordingly, and of the reasons why, and any member state that subsequently decides to grant a licence should first consult the partner which had originally refused.

Critics have observed that the Code is not legally binding, and have argued that the specific criteria in relation to denial of equipment that could support human rights abuse and internal repression are too loose. A further weakness is said to be the lack of any obligatory public statement that a licence has been refused, though it remains open to a state to apply moral pressure by disclosing its own refusal if it believes that another state is about to acquiesce.

There has in the UK been a time-honoured lack of specificity about the details of individual defence export contracts, justified at least as much by reference to commercial as to state secrecy. Attention was drawn to this issue in 1996 in the Scott report, which asked:

> Is it any longer satisfactory that Parliament and the British public are not entitled to be told to which countries and in what quantities goods such as artillery shells, land mines and cluster bombs have been licensed for export? ... the extent to which information on the export of arms and defence-related goods from this country can "in the public interest" properly be withheld from the public of this country should be the subject of public debate and further Government clarification (Scott Report, K 8, pp. 13-14; cited in Saferworld 1996, p. 7).

It is of interest, therefore, and a sign of further government action on this front, that it was reported in October 1998 that the FCO, DTI, and MOD were to publish in November the first of a new annual statement giving unprecedented detail of arms exports approvals. This report was, for the first time, going to spell out the types of arms-related equipment provided by British companies to particular countries. The significance of this step is that in the past, because equipment is grouped under sweeping categories, it has been difficult to distinguish between, for example, aircraft and parachutes. However, concluded the press report:

> The DTI and MOD successfully resisted Foreign Office pressure to disclose extensive information about export licences which had been refused, on the grounds it would provide valuable information to foreign defence companies (*Financial Times*, 16 October 1998).

This would, of course, also be the key information needed to establish categorically the extent of any change in practice. If correct, the reservation also seems a little odd: not only would the report be retrospective but, more importantly, under the terms of the EU Code member states should notify each other when they refuse an export licence. In formal terms that means notification of the governments of the EU members states, but it would stretch credulity to imagine that this news would not reach interested companies.

CONCLUSIONS

In terms of practical policy steps, therefore, we may say that a stronger rhetorical line is now being taken by the UK government over the control of arms exports; that it has played a significant role in bringing into being the EU Code; and that it has promised greater transparency over UK arms exports.[3] It behooves critics to show a little patience with a government that, at the time of writing, was only 19 months into the job. Nevertheless, it will have disappointed many to learn in November 1998 that the promised first annual report on arms exports had been delayed, apparently because of difficulty in assembling the data with the degree of transparency required by ministers, and that its new publication date was uncertain (*Financial Times*, 12 November 1998).

Implicit in these developments is a long-standing debate between those who argue that "if we don't sell, someone else will," and those who instead claim the moral high ground for a position that sees no justification for many, if not most, arms sales. A potentially fruitful perspective on this debate can be offered by current discussions among international relations theorists on the subject of "good international citizenship." This discussion stems, at least in part, from the sense that globalization, as well as the forces that underpin or unleash it (depending on your point of view), requires balancing by a renewed attention to the cultivation of international society.

Following the line proposed in a recent paper by Wheeler and Dunne (1998), we may first identify a realist position that argues, in security terms, that we cannot afford the luxury of propagating liberal values in an uncertain and dangerous world. An alternative view, however, argues that true security can only be born out of a recognition of mutual interdependence between the provision of national security, the strengthening of the international order, and the promotion of human rights. As these authors argue: "Good international citizenship moderates the realist struggle for power by strengthening the rules and norms of international order" (ibid., p. 854).

We might add that issues such as global warming, drug trafficking, and the management of refugees further add to the reasons for seeing international cooperation not as starry-eyed idealism but as enlightened self-interest.

How might these ideas be applied to the question of control of arms exports? First, they reinforce traditional arguments for caution. Arms once sold are available for use, and are usually mobile. Second, Wheeler and Dunne cite a criterion for action proposed by Linklater for judging the priority to be accorded when justifiable goals clash. According to this criterion, a state should *not* be expected to sacrifice its own vital security interests, but should otherwise "place the survival of [international] order before the satisfaction of minimal national advantages" (Linklater, cited in Wheeler and Dunne 1998, p. 855).[4] A choice, on these grounds, not to issue a licence may leave a government with an economic and social problem, arising from loss of business and threat to jobs. But making hard choices, and balancing the consequences of foreign and domestic policies, is surely the essence of government.

To say this is not, therefore, to imagine that there are likely to be cost-free or easy decisions in this field. It is, however, to suggest that there is a distinction between Utopian realism and practical idealism, and that the choice should usually fall to the latter.

NOTES

1. It was notable at the November 1998 Canada-UK Colloquium, where this chapter was first presented, that exception was taken by some participants to the use in this context of the term "subsidy." At the same time, those who took this view also accepted that various aspects of MOD expenditure had had some effect, difficult though it might be to quantify, upon the competitiveness of British defence firms. An illuminating observation came from Robert Wolfe, who suggested that we might reflect on the way that subsidy features in GATT debates. Perhaps we have here one of those irregular verbs, according to which I engage in reasonable practices, but you, he, she, and it "subsidize."

2. Implementation of the manifesto commitment took the form first of a green paper (UK. MOD 1998*a*), and then of a decision to launch the DDA as part of DERA, with the emphasis upon supporting technology transfer to the civil sector, announced on 5 November 1998.

3. In terms of transparency in the weapons field, we may also acknowledge the unprecedented frankness over fissile material stocks, as itemized in the Strategic Defence Review.

4. It is worth recalling that the costs of the 1991 Gulf War have been estimated at US$ 100 billion, far more than the profits from arms exports to Iraq over the preceding two decades.

REFERENCES

Gummett, P. and J. Reppy, eds. 1998. *The Relations Between Defence and Civil Technologies.* Dordrecht: Kluwer.

Gummett P. and J. Stein, eds. 1997. *European Defence Technology in Transition.* Amsterdam: Harwood.

Krause, K. 1992. *Arms and the State: Patterns of Military Production and Trade.* Cambridge: Cambridge University Press.

Labour Party. 1995. *Strategy for a Secure Future: Labour's Approach to the Defence Industry.* London: The Labour Party.

Miller, D. 1996. *Export or Die: Britain's Defence Trade with Iran and Iraq.* London: Cassell.

Oxford Research Group. 1998. *Government Subsidy of Arms Exports* (preliminary paper). Oxgord: ORG.

Saferworld. 1996. *The Scott Report: Implications for UK Export Policy.* London: Saferworld.

Spear, J. 1995. *Carter and Arms Sales: Implementing the Carter Administration's Arms Transfer Restraint Policy.* Basingstoke: Macmillan.

Stockholm International Peace Research Institute (SIPRI). 1998. *SIPRI Yearbook 1998: Armaments, Disarmament and International Security.* Oxford: Oxford University Press.

United Kingdom. Ministry of Defence. 1996. *Statement on the Defence Estimates 1996,* Cm 3223. London: HMSO.

_____ 1998a. *Defence Diversification: Getting the Most out of Defence Technology,* Cm3861. London: HMSO.

_____ 1998b. *The Strategic Defence Review,* Cm 3999. London: HMSO.

Wheeler, N.J. and T. Dunne. 1998. "Good International Citizenship: A Third Way for British Foreign Policy," *International Affairs*, 74(4):847-70.

12

The Politics, Economics and Ethics of Arms Exports: Making Sense of (Canadian) Sovereignty in a Post-Westphalian World

Claire Turenne Sjolander

> The modern state system is not based on some timeless principle of sovereignty, but on the production of a normative conception that links authority, territory, population (society, nation), and recognition in a unique way and in a particular place (the state). Attempting to realize this ideal entails a great deal of hard work on the part of statespersons, diplomats, and intellectuals: to establish and police practices consistent with the ideal, its components, and the links between them; to delegitimate and quash challenges or threats; and to paper over persistent anomalies to make them appear to be consistent with the ideal or temporary divergences from the diachronic trajectory toward a pristine Westphalian ideal. The ideal of sovereignty is a product of the actions of powerful agents and the resistances to those actions by those located at the margins of power (Biersteker and Weber 1996, p. 3).

INTRODUCTION

In this era hallmarked by both the economic restructuring inherent in globalization and by the demise of Cold War rivalries, it is less than surprising to find scholars asking themselves about the contemporary relevance of the idea of sovereignty. If borders are increasingly permeable, and the state's economic role has evolved toward that of facilitating the adaptation of national economies to the exigencies of a newly constructed global economy made up of mostly private agents, where do we find the Westphalian ideal of a state system as the exclusive centrepiece of world order? If post-Cold War conflicts are driving new reflections on the meaning and practice of security (from human to environmental), as well as conditioning the emergence of new threats (increasingly defined in subnational, and often non-state, terms), what is the pertinence of sovereignty as the organizing concept of world order stability?

Biersteker and Weber point to the tremendous energies expended in constructing the ideal of state sovereignty in both academic theory and in empirical "real world" practice. Through an examination of the economics and politics of defence production, and of the emergent restructuring of investment and trade patterns within these industrial sectors, this chapter highlights the paradoxes and contradictions — many of them ethical — of defence industries and the policies designed to govern them in a world clinging tenaciously to the principles of a state system that may well be a figment of our collective past.

Globalization, at least in its economic manifestations, constructs a "post-Westphalian" state logic. The perceived inescapability of the neo-liberal mantra of market liberalization has defined a new terrain for state and industry behaviour. Borders matter little, and diminishing their importance is directly correlated to economic competitiveness and to global success. As Alexander Murphy has observed, "the spatial structure of the international economy is to some degree at odds with the modern state system" (Murphy 1996, p. 107). The paradox, of course, is that (national) defence industries are, in their very nature, profoundly Westphalian constructions. The reasons are obvious: "[m]ost governments ... treat the ability to make weapons almost as seriously as the ability to use them, and will cede neither to foreigners" (*Economist* 1995b). National security is at stake if production is not nationally based and, thereby, controlled. In consequence, "[a] defence industry, rather like a currency, can turn into a kind of national virility symbol" (*Economist* 1997a). Without sovereign state borders, the existence and legitimacy of defence industries would not have been defined in terms of the state and of state sovereignty. This is not to argue, of course, that defence industries would not have emerged, but rather that they would not have been part of the *national* security apparatus.

While such an observation might seem at once profoundly obvious, and therefore trite, the national security calculus that once dominated national defence industries is beginning to change, however slowly, with the end of the Cold War. The economic restructuring that has characterized globalization is now slowly beginning to affect the production activities of defence industries, along the lines of the restructuring that began in many civilian manufacturing industries during the economic crisis of the 1970s. There is an important difference, however. These civilian industries were only rarely seen as national champions, much less national security champions. The coming globalization of the defence industries poses a new series of challenges that can be defined in terms of the eclipse of the Westphalian state system. What are the consequences for national, and indeed global, security of the growing non-coincidence between national sovereign boundaries and the territories that circumscribe defence industry production?

It should be noted that while this chapter will discuss the Canadian experience with respect to the post-Cold War restructuring of defence industries, it will do so within the broader perspective of the globalization of defence industries. It would in fact be an error to focus exclusively upon the Canadian experience, for current Canadian policies and practices with respect to defence production cannot be understood unless they are situated within the wider context of the restructuring of defence production, both continentally and within the Western alliance. In addition, it is particularly important to situate the Canadian experience more broadly due to the peculiar nature (in light of the comments above) of defence production in Canada.

Since 1940, with the conclusion the Ogdensburg agreement between the governments of Canada and the United States, Canadian defence policy has been formally defined in terms of continental security. While this agreement heralded the formal beginnings of Canada-US cooperation in matters of mutual and continental defence, such cooperation took another step forward in 1959, with the establishment of the Defence Production Sharing Arrangement (DPSA). This arrangement "allowed Canadian firms to compete on an equal footing with their American counterparts in the US market" (Canada 1994). Building upon this arrangement, the Defence Development Sharing Arrangement (DDSA) concluded in 1963 assisted Canadian firms in developing goods for use by the US military. In essence, therefore, while Canadian defence production could hardly have been said to have been "globalized" with the agreements in 1959 and 1963, such production certainly was "continentalized."

National security in the Canadian case, in respect both of strategic and of defence production considerations, was and remains formally equated with continental security. Unsurprisingly, therefore, restructuring in the Canadian defence sector has followed in large measure the restructuring evident in the American, and to a lesser extent, the European context. Notwithstanding the peculiar nature of Canadian defence production, the key questions of the post-Cold War era remain. Can industries established to provide the tools of national (or continental) security do so when they begin to cease to operate primarily along national lines or to serve their own sovereign national markets? What contradictions arise when the weapons of national security, that most Westphalian of constructs, are provided by industries that define the world in increasingly post-Westphalian terms?

THE MULTIPLE LOGICS OF GLOBALIZATION

The economic crisis that struck industrial economies in the early 1970s encouraged the restructuring of many sectors within civilian manufacturing production. This restructuring became one of the first concrete manifestations of what we now commonly call "globalization." Where firms had first exported their products in order to penetrate foreign markets and thus to secure market share, and where some had later established branch plants directly *in* foreign markets in order to produce and sell their wares there (thus securing not only market share, but market access if there were barriers to trade), they now began to change their production strategies in some of the sectors made vulnerable by the generalized reduction in demand in Western industrial economies.

Globalization has come to mean many things over the past three decades; nevertheless, it must at the outset be understood as a set of global economic processes that reflected this change in production strategies — a change set underway by the responses of transnational corporations to the economic downturn of the 1970s. For the first time, significant numbers of large companies began to conceive of primarily *national* lines of production in *international* terms, setting into motion a strategy of delocalization, or the internationalization, of production. In order to take advantage of less costly factor inputs abroad (cheaper labour, for example), or to position themselves more advantageously in foreign markets, firms divided their production processes across different national jurisdictions, consolidated their production (and market share) through mergers and acquisitions, and reinvigorated their export strategies. If the economically depressed markets of the Western countries could not provide enough consumers for the quantity of goods being produced by firms there, the latter could seek cheaper factor inputs into production abroad, reorienting their strategies to serve an international marketplace rather than a primarily domestic one.

These strategic responses to the economic crisis did not, of course, develop in a political vacuum. The global multilateral financial and trade institutions (the International Monetary Fund, the World Bank, the GATT, and now the World Trade Organization) had developed a regulatory regime facilitating the ease and security with which goods and capital could flow across international boundaries. In this sense, the economic restructuring we understand to have been at the origin of economic globalization would not have been as possible in the context of national regulation and high barriers to trade and investment. The political ground work of post-World War II economic liberalization, combined with the competitive spread of standardized systems and technologies of production, as well as advances in transportation and communications technologies, hastened the transformation of the international economy.

Along with a few other industrial sectors, however, defence industries were spared these pressures. National and international political practices and agreements limited or regulated the export practices of firms in the defence sector, limited or forbade foreign investors from participating in any meaningful way in the ownership structure of these firms, and regulated through government contracts the number and diversity of national firms. National security was the mantra that justified the exclusion of defence industries from the liberalized trading regime of the post-1945 world. Put most starkly, the question was asked: "How can you trust foreigners to provide you with the means of defence in an uncertain world?" (*Economist* 1995*a*). As the pressures of economic globalization began to "shake down" civilian industries, the resurgence of the Cold War in the early years of the Reagan administration enhanced the justification of protecting defence industries on grounds of national security.

The political implications of economic restructuring, or globalization, were and are very real. If competition for markets and investment dollars is the guiding principle of the new economy, states must be conscious of the regulatory environment they do, or do not, provide. Inattentiveness may mean that national firms lose their "competitive edge," or that international firms refuse to invest. Economic restructuring brings with it a new perception of the real constraints on political action. In responding to a post-World War II political thrust of economic liberalization, economic globalization has pushed forward that agenda into the terrain of the inevitable. Particularly since the collapse of the Soviet Union and the Eastern bloc, globalization has taken on the aura of the inescapable.

The global diffusion of neo-liberalism, for better or worse, makes it appear that the alternatives are non-existent: jump on the globalization bandwagon, or lose out. "Competitiveness," "efficiency," "liberalization," the "minimalist state" — these have become the buzzwords of this new political discourse. In highlighting the inevitability of restructuring, globalization is portrayed as a set of processes beyond the realm of politics. Firms must adapt to the new realities in order to compete and to secure market share in an increasingly global economy, and states must facilitate this transition, or globalization will leave them behind. Whether or not this is actually the case is in some respects a moot point. What is important is that states behave as though it were the case, and accept that they must facilitate the economic competitiveness that has become the new rule of the game.

It was within this new economic setting that the Cold War breathed its last. Suddenly, the requirement for massive defence procurement budgets was thrown into question, and political leaders began to dream of the programs made possible if they could only cash in on the "peace dividend." Despite the Gulf War, global defence spending dropped from $1.2 trillion in 1985 (at the height of the renewed Cold War) to $868 billion in 1993 (in constant 1993 prices) (*Economist* 1996).

When one considers the escalating costs of developing and manufacturing new generations of weapons systems, the fall in defence spending becomes all the more noteworthy. Defence industries are now confronting the same pressures of a rapidly diminishing national market as civilian industries did decades earlier. Unsurprisingly, their responses are similar. Richard Bitzinger explains: "[a]s military spending around the world declines and defense industries face major contractions in their national arms markets, 'going global' in arms production has become a critical corporate and government strategy for ensuring the preservation and economic viability of national defense industrial bases" (Bitzinger 1994, p. 171).

The same pressures — to increase export markets, to consolidate market share through mergers and acquisitions, and to engage in strategies of delocalized production through joint venture agreements or active foreign investment abroad — have been defining the environment for defence industries in the post-Cold War era. This environment is being formed according to the "leaner, meaner" competitive principle so familiar in other sectors of the economy for the past three decades. The globalization thrust, however, blurs the national lines and sovereign borders that have justified and supported national defence industries for decades if not centuries. Globalization teaches that these firms have no other options in order to remain competitive and viable, and states, including the Canadian state, have become active supporters of this economic restructuring.

EXPORTS GALORE: DEFENCE INDUSTRIES "GO GLOBAL"

The close relationship between government and defence industries has meant, in large part, that states have been key players in encouraging defence firms to begin to move into the global marketplace. States are, after all, the major legitimate purchasers of weapons systems, and as such, have played a key role in nurturing the development of those industries. Once national markets began to shrink, substitutes had to be found — or an entire industry would find itself in crisis. Importantly, given the extent to which Canadian defence production is integrated with that of the US, the formal and very public drive toward the international marketplace (and international marketing) began in the 1992 American presidential election. During the campaign, George Bush announced a $6-billion sale of 150 F-16 fighter aircraft to Taiwan. As *The Economist* noted only somewhat tongue-in-cheek, "[l]est the point be missed, Mr. Bush spoke in front of a banner reading 'Jobs for America – Thanks Mr. President'." Exports of fighter aircraft to a potential global trouble spot were to be celebrated because they would preserve the health of the American economy. National security in the post-Cold War era became defined in a pointedly different way. The Democrats proved no different;

Bill Clinton approved of the sale to Taiwan, and, three weeks before Bush officially announced it, celebrated the sale of 72 F-15s (a larger tactical fighter than the F-16) to Saudi Arabia for a total of $9 billion on the deal (*Economist* 1994*a*). By 1995, despite the protests of liberal Democrats, the export push became official US government policy. In February, a presidential directive formally acknowledged the relationship between arms exports and the health of the defence industries. It defined "one objective of US defence exports as enhancing 'the ability of the US defence industrial base to meet US defence requirements and maintain long-term military technological superiority at lower costs'." In 1996, the Clinton administration engineered an export-financing program for defence contractors. With the launch of this new program, the US Treasury agrees, for a fee, to back commercial loans to countries wishing to buy American military equipment, up to a total of $15 billion (*Economist* 1997*b*).

US arms sales have become an important way by which the American defence industry remains competitive and viable: by 1993, US defence producers had succeeded in capturing a 70-percent share of the global arms market, compared to 21 percent in 1989. While the international arms market is obviously very volatile, and one enormous sale can clearly skew the figures for a given year, the greater presence of US defence firms in the global marketplace cannot be understood as the product of sheer happenstance.

This is not to argue that there are no export-control regimes seeking to regulate the sale of weapons systems to potentially dangerous purchasers. The fact remains, however, that the main purchasers of weapons systems are those who most anticipate a use for them, and so it is unremarkable that Egypt, Israel, Kuwait, South Korea, Greece, Turkey, Saudi Arabia, and Taiwan rank among America's best customers. Ethical considerations can too easily become the first victims of the drive to capture international arms markets, particularly as that international market shrinks in size. This is nowhere more starkly illustrated than in the comment made by Joel Johnson, vice-president of the Aerospace Industries Association, in response to the possibility of Congressionally mandated restrictions on arms sales to states that oppress their own populations: "There's something wrong with the whole policy because of a couple of strafing runs over Turkish villages?" (*Economist* 1994*a*).

The Canadian government has adopted similar practices to try to maintain the viability of its branch-plant defence sector. With the decline of the US as Canada's most significant market for weapons exports, Ottawa has encouraged the diversification of export markets for Canadian military production. It must be noted that annual figures for Canadian exports of military equipment are inevitably volatile, and depend heavily upon the impact of individual large sales. Despite this, a number of trends can be observed. First, in spite of the downturn in the global market for defence products, Canadian military equipment producers have been seeking a greater range of opportunities for sale abroad. The Department of Foreign Affairs and International Trade (DFAIT), for example, has noted that between 1990 and 1996, Canadian defence producers increased their export penetration from 50 countries to 99 (although there was a notable drop back to 69 countries in 1997) (Métivier 1999).

Second, Ottawa has sought to identify potential markets that might prove most lucrative for Canadian defence exporters. The 1996 report, *Canada's International Business Strategy 1996-1997: Aerospace and Defence*, notes that the "major area of growth in demand over the next few years is expected to be the Pacific Rim" (Canada 1996, p. 5). Further, a 1995 government report promises support for increasing military exports to Asia-Pacific countries. The strategy will "provide Canadian suppliers with unique export assistance ... to assist them in exploiting emerging markets in the Asia-Pacific and Middle East regions" (Canada 1995, p. 5). As Project Ploughshares has documented, Ottawa

> has been as good as its word. Recent efforts to boost military sales to Asia-Pacific have included: support from the crown corporations the Canadian Commercial Corporation (CCC) and the Export Development Corporation (for example, the CCC brokered a $146-million transport helicopter deal with the Thailand Army in 1994); active participation of the Department of National Defence, especially through equipment demonstrations and training (Canadian soldiers have trained Thai personnel on the ADATS missile system); hosting of foreign military missions to Canada ...; and government-sponsored promotional booths at international aerospace and military shows, in the region ... and at the biennial Airshow Canada exhibition at Abbotsford, BC.... More prominently, government Cabinet ministers, including the Prime Minister, have led trade missions to the region that have included military industry representatives (Project Ploughshares 1996*a*).

Of course, these assessments raise the question of whether there is anything particularly offensive about government support for the export market diversification of an important industrial base. After all, there are export controls on military goods, contained in law in the Export Control List (ECL) under Group 2 (Munitions). Group 2 lists goods that are "specifically designed or modified for military use." Under the guidelines, Canada controls the export of military goods and technology to countries that:

> a) pose a threat to Canada and its allies; b) are involved in or under imminent threat of hostilities; c) are under United Nations Security Council sanctions; and d) have governments that have a persistent record of serious violations of the human rights of their citizens, unless it can be demonstrated that there is no reasonable risk that the goods might be used against the civilian population (Canada. DFAIT 1997).

The problem arises when the guidelines are applied in what might be considered less than stringent fashion. For example, in 1994, Canada exported military goods to 34 developing nations, of which fully 18 were identified by Amnesty International as guilty of significant human rights violations, and in Ruth Sivard's report on *"World Military and Social Expenditures"* as practising frequent violence against their own populations (Project Ploughshares 1995). This difficulty was implicitly acknowledged when, in June 1996, Foreign Affairs Minister Lloyd Axworthy instructed his department to "do more rigorous analyses of security issues and threats of hostilities... and internal conflicts such as civil wars" and to "give a stricter interpretation of the human rights criteria, including increased requirements for end-use assurances to minimize the risk that Canadian equipment would fall into the hands of those that might use it to abuse human rights" (Canada. DFAIT 1997).

Despite this, in 1996, Canada shipped military goods to governments involved in major human rights violations and to countries suffering from internal wars (Epps 1998*a*; Thompson 1997). While arms exports did decline in 1997 (the last year for which figures are available), destinations continued to include such countries as Egypt, Turkey, Peru, and Kenya — all of which have been beset by internal conflicts — and Saudi Arabia, Brazil, and Thailand, where human rights violations by security forces have been well documented (Epps 1998*b*). Whether or not the decline in military exports is due to more stringent application of the export control guidelines, or simply to normal, but often considerable, fluctuations in arms sales, remains an open question.

In addition to concerns over the application of Canada's export control regime, there is also the question of the "invisible" military trade. Because the ECL's military classification is determined by virtue of a product's technical characteristics, rather than by end-use, military goods "are specified without reference to export customer" (Project Ploughshares 1996*b*). Combined with the growing promotion of "dual-use" technologies and a concomitant procurement strategy (adopted both in Canada and the US), an export control regime that enables products to be classified as civilian whatever their intended end-use is necessarily problematic.

For example, the sale in 1994 of Bell 212 helicopters to the Colombian armed forces did not have to be authorized by the Canadian export control system. Although the helicopters were originally developed for the military, the Bell 212s had received civilian certification, and could therefore be exported as commercial (non-military) aircraft. In essence, "[t]he helicopters could be bought by military customers, and they could be used for military operations, but they were not military goods as found on the ... Export Control List" (Project Ploughshares 1996*b*). Although ECL Group 1 (Dual Use) was developed in order to take into account "strategically important goods with significant potential to enhance military capability" (Canda. DFAIT 1998), as with Group 2 products, careful vigilance that is sensitive to the buyer and the intended likely usage of the product is necessary in order adequately to evaluate the appropriateness of the sale. A preoccupation with facilitating the acquisition of new export markets is not the best guide for application of the criteria.

THE MERGER AND ACQUISITION FRENZY

Where a concern with export markets and the promotion of military exports has characterized one pillar of the "going global" strategy, it is by no means the only such pillar. As was the case with civilian industries many years earlier, the depressed market for arms sales has encouraged a frenzy of mergers and acquisitions — an attempt to "grow" firms large enough to become behemoths within a global military market. Defence "giants" have been created not solely by market forces, but have responded to political conditions propitious to their development.

In 1993, in what is now referred to as the famous "Last Supper," then US Defense Secretary Les Aspin and his deputy, William Perry, invited a dozen defence industry chiefs to attend a dinner in the Pentagon, hosted by the latter. Perry told the assembled guests that there were twice as many of them in the room as he wanted to see in five years' time, and that the US government was prepared to watch some of them go out of business. Combined with the judicious application of subsidies designed to facilitate mergers (US defence companies have been able to claim reimbursements for the costs of mergers), and the relaxation of the government's antitrust policy (which until 1998 had been rarely used to block defence mergers), consolidation in the US defence industry was achieved at a dizzying pace.

Between 1992 and 1997, a total of $55 billion in military industry mergers took place, according to the Securities Data Company (Wayne 1998). From 15 major defence contractors at the beginning of the 1990s, there remained but three giants by 1997: Boeing, Lockheed Martin, and Raytheon. While Washington finally did object to the merger of Lockheed Martin and Northrop Grumman (the distant fourth-place military contractor), the impressive restructuring and consolidation of important segments of the defence industry had already been achieved.

Such a pattern of mergers and acquisitions has been far less obvious in Western Europe, where the plenitude of national boundaries, coupled with an enthusiasm for "national security" as a form of protectionism, has dampened prospects of consolidation. Preferences for home-grown defence suppliers in Britain, France, and Germany, as well as restrictions against foreign ownership of top defence contractors, has necessarily implied that cross-boundary mergers to achieve economies of scale have been much more difficult. The European preference has favoured cross-border joint ventures — such as those linking Germany's Siemens with Britain's Plessey in defence electronics, and the latter's Shorts with France's Thompson-CSF in missiles (*Economist* 1994*b*). Attempts at collaborative development of new weapons systems, such as the Eurofighter (a joint research and development venture between Germany, Britain, Italy, and Spain), have so far proven costly. The difficulty of such endeavours has begun to encourage a greater degree of industry consolidation, motivated in part by concern that European firms will not be able to compete for international markets against the American giants.

By contrast, the wave of American consolidations has had relatively little impact on Canada. Although changes in the Canadian defence industry have reflected the restructuring of parent companies, "most have exerted little to no influence on the upper echelons of Canada's military manufacturers" (Epps 1998*c*). Within the ranks of the top ten military contractors in Canada, the only new entrant by the close of 1997 was Magellan Aerospace Corporation. Magellan achieved its lofty heights by virtue of its acquisition of Winnipeg-based Bristol Aerospace and Orenda Aerospace (formerly Hawker-Siddeley Canada) of Mississauga. To the extent that the Canadian defence industry is continentally integrated, and that the major US players are not key firms within the Canadian context (none of Boeing, Lockheed Martin, or Raytheon figure among the largest defence contractors in Canada), the recent spate of mergers and acquisitions that has reshaped the US defence industry has had only second-order effects on Canadian defence producers. A similar push to home-grown mergers and acquisitions has not occurred within Canada, a fact unsurprising given that the Canadian industry is, by and large, not "Canadian."

DELOCALIZATION ON THE HORIZON

If the pattern of industrial restructuring that characterized civilian industries as they confronted the effects of the economic crisis holds, defence industries are now poised to move to a strategy of delocalization. In part, the focus on dual-use technologies and the increased reliance of defence contractors on civilian suppliers make this inevitable. The shrinking international defence market, and the importance of specialized high technology systems, is driving this inevitability.

> Slowly but surely, the defence industry is becoming more like any other. With advances in weaponry driven by commercial technologies such as digital communications and microelectronics, there is now more spin-on from the civilian economy to defence than spin-off from it. Weapons factories and research laboratories are less cut off from the mainstream economy than they used to be. To save money, defence ministries [including the Canadian Department of National Defence] are making

contractors use cheaper, off-the-shelf commercial components instead of specially designed military ones, and that means defence companies have more foreign subcontractors (*Economist* 1997*a*).

As the chairman of Lockheed Martin, Norman R. Augustine, expressed it, "[w]e will have American industry providing for national defense. But we will not have a national defense industry.... We'll have to draw on our industrial base rather than having the defense capability of the past" (Wayne 1998, p. D1). Though there remains a national reluctance, whatever the economic imperatives, to encourage "national champion" defence industries to participate fully in the globalization game, no similar impediment exists for civilian suppliers of defence industries, or indeed, in most cases, for suppliers of dual-use technologies. To that extent, internationalization strategies have already made themselves felt within the defence sector, albeit through an (increasingly significant) back door.

Even within the leading-edge defence sector, however, explicit moves toward greater international production and cooperation have become more common. Richard Bitzinger outlines the industrial strategies that make up the first wave of globalization within defence industries, namely co-production agreements (defined as the joint manufacture of a weapons system originally developed in one country), and co-development programs (where governments or multinational corporate teams work together to jointly develop and manufacture a weapons system). Where co-production and co-development programs have tended to be restricted to Western industrialized countries and their defence producers, they are gradually becoming more prevalent in arms production in certain developing countries.

Taiwan's Indigenous Defence Fighter is the result of close collaboration with several US defence firms, while the Korean K-1 tank draws heavily upon the expertise of US firms in design and systems integration, along with imports of Western weapons technology (Bitzinger 1994, p. 179). The US has participated in a number of significant arms sales involving important co-production offsets, including Israel (the F-15 and F-16 fighters), Korea (the F-16 fighter and the P-3 patrol aircraft), Singapore, Greece, Indonesia, Taiwan (the F-16 fighter), as well as Canada and Spain (the F/A-18 fighter). While the movement to delocalization and similar globalization strategies remains limited, there is clear and growing evidence that defence industries will follow the lead of their civilian industry predecessors.

This is particularly the case if Bitzinger is correct in his assessment that the number of private-sector initiatives for international arms collaboration has increased dramatically. Faced with a stagnation of government-led initiatives, industry-to-industry defence collaboration has grown considerably. Since the mid-1980s, defence companies have increased the number of privately funded transnational research and development programs, including the NASAMS advanced surface-to-air missile system (a joint project between Hughes Aircraft Company and NFT of Norway), and the APACHE standoff munition (a private venture between two French companies, Matra and Aérospatiale, and Germany's Deutsche Aerospace [DASA]) (Bitzinger 1994, p. 181). Since the end of the Cold War, the number of joint ventures and strategic alliances between foreign defence firms has increased substantially, and with the declining role of government in launching new R&D programs in the defence sector, such interfirm private cooperation is expected to increase.

CONCLUSIONS: ETHICAL IMPLICATIONS OF ERODING SOVEREIGNTY

Security or markets and the security of markets — in many respects, this is the challenge confronting states today as defence industries begin the move into the post-Westphalian order. Defence industries are invariably defined as leading-edge industries that provide access to emerging technologies, and create significant numbers of high technology jobs for those countries that are able to sustain them. Canada is no exception to this rule, and in the post-Cold War era, its long-established defence production relationship with the United States is heralded for the advantages it provides in a context of diminished resources and increased competition. Whatever the benefits to national or continental security, "[t]hese arrangements ... allow Canadian firms to stay in touch with developing technologies and help Canada generate and sustain high-technology jobs in the defence and civilian sectors" (Canada 1994). "Competitiveness," "efficiency," and "jobs, jobs, jobs" are intrinsically linked to the need to protect defence industries. Within the logics of globalization, however, such protection can only be afforded if firms become internationally competitive, and position themselves in the global marketplace.

A concern for markets and jobs, however, brings with it some political, and ethical, implications. It is difficult, at best, to define a comprehensive post-Cold War export control regime,[1] a task made more difficult by the search for markets. For example, the US sale of F-16s to Taiwan so infuriated China that it left the post-Gulf War talks about arms-transfers controls. Attempting to deal with the issue of international arms sales is hampered when the architects of such attempts are themselves seeking to capture a larger share of the international arms market. As we have seen in the Canadian case, even where export control regulations do exist, the blurring between civilian and defence industries, the growth of dual-use technologies, and the difficulty of interpreting end-use intentions make the effective operation of such regimes problematic — all the more so if at the same time, the same state is committed to facilitating export growth in its defence sector. Fuelling regional instability (or, at a minimum, creating the conditions by which such instability can become more lethal) through the infusion of weapons because governments and defence industries are searching for markets shines the spotlight brightly on the security-versus-markets question.

Despite the important issues relating to the defence sector's global export drive, it is not here that the more difficult paradoxes arise. Co-production or co-development arrangements almost inevitably imply some form of technology transfer. Such transfers have already permitted certain countries with a "no questions asked" policy when it comes to arms sales (notably Brazil and Israel) to develop their indigenous defence industries to the point where they have become important exporters of arms. The development of a second tier of arms exporters, who are also experiencing the pressures of a shrinking international arms market, heightens competition for markets, and increases the push to sell, even if the longer term implications are less than clear.

More fundamentally, the increased tendency to adopt globalization strategies means that the control of exports is in some respects impossible, and potentially moot. Globally produced goods, through networks of international subcontractors, joint ventures, and strategic alliances (not to mention mergers and acquisitions), make it more difficult to identify the "nationality" of a particular weapon. Just as civilian corporations have been able to transfer assets between jurisdictions in order to advantage their shareholders and increase their profits, defence industries stand poised to do the same. Anything short of a universal export control regime will not defend national, or global, security interests. To reiterate the words of Alexander Murphy, "the spatial structure of the international economy is to some degree at odds with the modern state system," (Murphy 1996, p. 107) and this non-coincidence can be particularly challenging, and potentially dangerous, where defence industries are concerned. "[I]nternational arms collaboration, involving as it does the permanent share-out of resources, skills, and technology that underlie armaments production, is potentially more destabilizing than outright arms sales. These capabilities, once transferred, cannot be cut off or recovered" (Bitzinger 1994, p. 190).

The message is a sobering one. The reality remains, however, that there is no likely easy way out of the ethical paradox that this creates within the logics of globalization. If the internationalization of production is inevitable, defence industries are merely doing what they must, and states have no choice but to support such endeavours in order to remain competitive. State sovereignty in a post-Westphalian world is no guarantor of national, or international, security. It is only by coming to terms with the full implications of a globalizing world that a way out of the security-markets maze can be found. Unlike the imagined inevitabilities of globalization, however, on this score, we truly have no choice.

NOTE

1. In the wake of the Gulf War, there have been efforts to devise just such a regime. The 1996 Wassenaar Arrangement between 33 countries, including Canada, "seeks to ensure regional and international peace and security by preventing destabilizing accumulations of conventional weapons and dual-use equipment" (Canada. DFAIT 1998).

REFERENCES

Biersteker, T.J. and C. Weber. 1996. "The Social Construction of State Sovereignty," in *State Sovereignty as a Social Construct*, ed. T.J. Biersteker and C. Weber. Cambridge: Cambridge University Press.

Bitzinger, R.A. 1994. "The Globalization of the Arms Industry: The Next Proliferation Challenge," *International Security,* 19(2):170-202.

Canada. 1994. *1994 Defence White Paper*. Ottawa: Department of National Defence.

_____ 1995. *Canada's Export Strategy: The Industrial Trade Business Plan, 1995/96.* No. 11, *Defence Products*. Ottawa: Supply and Services Canada.

_____ 1996. *Canada's International Business Strategy 1996-1997: Aerospace and Defence*. Ottawa: Supply and Services Canada.

Canada. Department of Foreign Affairs and International Trade (DFAIT). 1997. "Export of Military Goods from Canada, Annual Report 1996." Ottawa: Export and Import Control Bureau. Http://www.dfaitmaeci.gc.ca/~EICB/export/Military/96/mil96front-e.htm. November.

_____ 1998. "Export of Military Goods from Canada, Annual Report 1997." Ottawa: Export and Import Control Bureau. Http://www.dfaitmaeci.gc.ca/~EICB/export/Military97/mil97front-e.htm. November.

The Economist. 1994a. "Arms Sales Boom," 13 August, p. 25.

_____ 1994b. "Heads in the Clouds," 3 September, p. 16.

_____ 1995a. "Attack the Frontiers," 8 April, p. 18.

_____ 1995b. "Markets and Maginot Lines." 28 October, p. 23.

_____ 1996. "American Monsters, European Minnows," 13 January, p. 63.

_____ 1997a. "Linking Arms," 14 June, p. 3.

_____ 1997b. "Land of the Giants," 14 June, p. 7.

Epps, Ken. 1998a. "More Canadian Arms to Human Rights Violators and Countries at War," *Ploughares Monitor*, March, pp. 3-6.

_____ 1998b. "Canada Reports Drop in Overseas Military Exports," *Ploughshares Monitor*, December, pp. 14-15.

_____ 1998c. "Canada's Largest Military Contractors," *Ploughshares Monitor*, December, pp. 17-18.

Métivier, C. 1999. "Évolution de l'idée de reconversion de l'industrie militaire au sein de l'État canadien," paper presented to the 67th congress of the Association canadienne française pour l'avancement des sciences, University of Ottawa, 14 May.

Murphy, A.B. 1996. "The Sovereign State System as Political-Territorial Ideal: Historical and Contemporary Considerations," in *State Sovereignty as a Social Construct*, ed. Biersteker and Weber.

Project Ploughshares. 1995. "Canadian Arms Sales to the Third World." *Ploughshares Monitor*. Http://www.ploughshares.ca/content/MONITOR/mons95a.html. September.

_____ 1996a. "Feeding the Tigers." *Ploughshares Monitor*. Http://www.ploughshares.ca/content/MONITOR/monj96b.html. June.

_____ 1996b. "Canada's Unrecorded Military Trade."*Ploughshares Monitor*. Http://www.ploughshares.ca/content/MONITOR/mons96d.html. September.

Thompson, A. 1997. "Canada Boosts Arms Exports to Third World: Some Nations on List Have Internal Conflicts," *Toronto Star*, 14 December.

Wayne, L. 1998. "The Shrinking Military Complex," *New York Times*, 27 February, pp. D1, D6.

PART FOUR

CONCLUSION

13

Conclusion

Denis Stairs

The subject of the 1998 Canada-UK Colloquium was encapsulated in its title: "Security, Strategy and the Global Economics of Defence Production." At the end of the proceedings, the topic itself may not have been completely exhausted, but certainly its dimensions had been fully canvassed. So had the background factors. These included:

- the general uncertainty of the strategic environment in the post-Cold War period;

- the impact of modern technology, especially *information* technology, on warfare and military procurement;

- the effect of globalization on the practices and behaviours of the components of the defence industrial base, and on government policies in response;

- the interaction between technological change and defence procurement on the one hand, and strategic doctrine (or, defence policy) on the other;

- the consequences of political and fiscal constraints for government spending; and

- the looming presence, as a kind of "immovable object," of the United States as a hegemonic power — a power to which everyone else, in one way or another, is forced to accommodate.

In this concluding chapter, I take these background factors in turn, seeking not to recapitulate the argument of the various chapters, but rather to provide the reader with the flavour of the discussion that they generated, when they were initially presented as papers at the Colloquium.

THE STRATEGIC ENVIRONMENT

The first of the contextual realities became very evident in the paper presented by Fen Hampson, which supplied a vivid account of the variety and complexity of the conflicts that seem now to plague the world community. It was impossible to absorb his analysis without acquiring a renewed sense of what might be called the "inevitability of eclecticism" in the international politics of our time.

This awareness carries with it a recognition of the difficulty of knowing which particular manifestation of human perversity in politics is going to reveal itself next on the international conflict agenda. And herein lies the policymaker's daunting dilemma. The Cold War, as one participant, Bruce George,[1] pointed out, had at least had the advantage of imparting a certain stability to the international political environment. This had made it possible to identify, with a reasonable measure of assurance, what the defence problems really were. On Hampson's assessment, however, everyone is left at sea, with little by way of a system of navigation from which to divine a course. It need hardly be said that this is not Hampson's fault; it is "reality," not Hampson's analysis, that is out of joint. And the consequence of that reality, as noted in another of George's observations, is that prudence, in an uncertain environment, requires the preservation of a significant capability for using force.

This view was reiterated, in different ways, by the two government ministers who spoke at lunch on the meeting's first day, 6 November 1998. In particular, Canadian Minister of National Defence Art Eggleton, observed that we now face an even greater variety of security threats than ever before, and that the problem is being gravely compounded by the escalating costs of rapidly changing military technology. UK Minister of State for the Armed Forces Douglas Henderson, made much the same point in the context of expressing his concern over the lack of public understanding of what the maintenance of security in the current international environment actually requires. In the follow-up discussion, Eggleton reported that the same lack of public recognition of the problem could be found in the Canadian context, as well. Among other things, it was reflected in a widespread reluctance to support expenditures on the Canadian Forces — a point that was reiterated later in the proceedings with particular reference to the role played in Canadian defence policy debates by the press.

In short, there seemed to be a general recognition that the world is still a violent place, that military interventions, however unhappily, will therefore be recurrent requirements in the future, that these interventions will take many different forms, and that this is a difficult message to convey convincingly to the public (especially, perhaps, in Canada, but also in the United Kingdom).

THE IMPACT OF TECHNOLOGY ON WARFARE AND PROCUREMENT

The impact of technology on warfare and procurement was a theme that not only pervaded the session on the so-called "revolution in military affairs" (or RMA), but also ran through the entire conference. With respect specifically to the RMA discussion, however, it was difficult not to conclude at the end that *all* arguments on the impact of technology on warfare and the armed forces are *partly* true, but that none of the arguments is true for every case or in every context. Once again, eclecticism appeared to be inevitable, and once again, the realities were shown to be untidy.

There can be little doubt that information technology affects almost everything that people in uniform do. This is hardly surprising. It is affecting everything that academics do, too! On the other hand, Neil MacFarlane's deep reservations about overstating the RMA case, and Thierry Gongora's cautious emphasis on the inherent incrementalism of the processes of technological change and on the consequent need to avoid making the final judgement on the implications too soon, both seemed to be very well taken. The more enthusiastic converts to "arcade"-style perceptions of the Gulf War and its "lessons" often appear, it must be said, alarmingly reminiscent of the McNamara "whiz kids" of some 30 years ago, with their complacent predictions of how the mightiest state in the history of humankind could use its superior technology to make short work of a remote peasant community in Indo-China. In the event, they were tragically disappointed, and there may be a case now for remembering the lessons of their experience.

One of those lessons is that war is ultimately about *politics* and about the attempt to influence political behaviour in a context in which the target is firmly committed to resist. That being so, "surgical strikes" may have a chance of doing the job in a few very limited cases, but not in most. Another is the lesson of the "paradox of power," to which MacFarlane's analysis implicitly alluded. In the real world, the "weak" are often surprisingly adept at defeating the "strong."

Whether, in short, "going high-tech" really helps, and if so, by how much, depends on what one is trying to accomplish, against whom, under what conditions, and for how long. None of those who were present for the discussion could have come away from it thinking that they had canvassed a simple problem, much less that they had uncovered simple answers.

THE EFFECT OF GLOBALIZATION ON THE DEFENCE INDUSTRIAL BASE

The impact of globalization on the operations of the defence industrial base again ran recurrently, both explicitly and implicitly, throughout the entire proceedings, and the "outsiders" at the table were rewarded with some fascinating glimpses of how the process works, and how the fault-line between what Claire Turenne Sjolander called the "political space" and the "economic space" is actually joined. Academic though she claimed her preoccupations to be, she put the observations of both the captains of industry and the architects of government in clear and telling perspective. But on this question, as on others, a final conclusion could not be discerned, and it remained unclear how the contest between the two spaces would be resolved in the end, and on what terms.

Among political scientists, of course, the entire question of the role, even the survivability, of the state in a globalizing world is currently a subject of hot debate. Some think that an entirely new structure of "regimes" is now under visible and rapid development, and that the days of the so-called Westphalian state system are clearly numbered. It will be replaced, on this account, by a much more complex array of problem-solving institutions, operating in layered webs and overlapping mosaics. In this evolution, the distinction between "public" and "private" will become increasingly blurred, while the connection between communal identity and sovereign polity gradually falls into decay. Because the defence function is so central to the most basic purpose of the state, and because it rests so firmly on the sovereignty principle, the problem of reconciling it with the globalizing "transnationalism" of the major commercial enterprises in the defence field represents a test case *par excellence*. There is an argument for watching its progress very closely, because it may be where the battle turns out to be most transparently joined. Its outcome, in other words, may tell us a great deal about where we, and the state system, are really going. The captains of the defence industrial establishment may not normally think of their enterprises as historical bellwethers, but in the present context, this could very well be what they are.

THE INTERACTION BETWEEN DEFENCE PROCUREMENT AND STRATEGIC DOCTRINE

On the question of the interaction between technological change and defence procurement on the one hand, and strategic doctrine on the other, it appeared at the outset that the Canadian and UK cases were very different, and that this difference was a function of power and scale. In essence, Canadian policy seemed to be driven by hardware, while British policy was driven by strategic calculus. That picture became less tidy, however, as the discussion unfolded, and by the end it appeared that the differences might be matters more of degree than of kind. They were *important* differences, no doubt, but not qualitatively so significant as initial inspection might suggest. Just as there is no escaping eclecticism in international affairs on matters of this kind, so there is no escaping the fact that almost everything interacts with almost everything else. Procurement decisions and strategic decisions, even for the greater powers, are components of a feedback loop.

Having said that, at least one point of contrast between the Canadian and UK cases seemed to come through "loud and clear." Specifically, in the field of defence procurement, Canada may well have been the first of the "globalizers." Canada has *never*, in fact, regarded the maintenance of a national defence industrial base as part of its *defence* policy. This has been a consequence of its relatively small size, when taken in combination with its secure geopolitical circumstances — circumstances that David Haglund was especially careful to highlight. Historically, Canada has always known that it would be protected, in the end, by someone else — by the British first, and then by the Americans.

There was a time, a brief time, when it actually produced, albeit selectively, complete major weapons platforms. It did so, for example, in World War II, when the task was economically feasible (given the technology of the day), and when it was a contribution to the conduct of the hostilities that Canadian politicians were particularly happy to make. It did so, as well, in the early period of the Cold War, when the undertaking seemed like good economic policy, good research and development (R&D) policy, and good "vanity politics." But when the escalating costs of military technology finally spent Ottawa out of the game, it simply stopped trying, and concentrated instead (as several of the participants pointed out) on the production of components, "bits and pieces," rather than entire systems.

This is a well-known tale, but one of its most interesting features is that no one in Canada has ever felt any less secure because of it. On the contrary, the easy acceptance of such necessities went back at least as far as the Hyde Park Agreement of World War II, and the Defence Production and Defence Development Sharing Arrangements with the United States in the late 1950s and early 1960s. Canadians were eager to negotiate these facilities; indeed, they initiated them. And for the most part (there was a brief period of controversy during the Vietnam War), they have warmly cherished the jobs, the profits, and the economies of scale that have ensued. Only with the Avro Arrow did they fleetingly flirt with a defence-procurement *politique de grandeur*. But even then there was not a single trace of Gaullist aspiration in either their ambitions, or in the *angst* that followed upon the Arrow's cancellation. It was, rather, the prestige of high-tech aero-engineering, along with the economic spin-offs that they hoped it would entail, that tickled their fancies most.

In the United Kingdom, by contrast, the discussion seemed to suggest that there were still traces, gradually fading though they might be, of the autarchic premise at work, at least where defence procurement is concerned. The capacity to "go it alone" is there thought to be itself a prerequisite of security, or at least a significant contributor to it. The thought of having to depend on other countries for the acquisition of military systems creates unease, as a kind of discomfiting by-product of economic interdependence. Perhaps this is one of the indicators of great power status. By contrast, middle powers resign themselves to their position and make the (economic) best of it.

THE CONSEQUENCES OF CONSTRAINTS ON GOVERNMENT SPENDING

The consequences of fiscal stress were clearly evident in the presentations of both of the government ministers, but they were reflected as well in the observations of many of the other participants. Both countries, in short, are acutely aware of their budgetary limitations.

Again, however, there was reason at the end to conclude that there is a step-order difference in the *scale* of the problem in the two cases. It was hard not to conclude that the expenditure run-down in Canada — especially in the case of the forces on the ground and in the air — has put the Canadians at the extreme margins of operational viability. The discussion effectively echoed the dark humour of Canadian army colonels, who have been known, with what they think is only slight exaggeration, to question their ability to put down a hockey riot in a medium-sized Canadian city! As Rear-Admiral D.E. Miller pointed out in the final session, the units of Maritime Command are somewhat better off, and they are now working closely with other sea-going fleets in the government apparatus to amplify their capabilities. But elsewhere the picture is a melancholy one, which is precisely what the level of Canada's annual defence expenditures (currently reported in the range of 1.2 percent of GDP) would lead the properly informed to expect.

This phenomenon is ultimately rooted in the widespread perception that Canada fundamentally lacks a genuine defence problem of its own, and that its principal capacity for making a meaningful contribution to international security comes by way of peacekeeping. Increasingly, moreover, the peacekeeping that Canadians have in mind is a process given over as much to an elaborate form of social work as to the direct containment of violence per se.

There was some indication in the discussion that the British defence establishment is now facing similar pressures. In the United Kingdom, however, there is a "great power" tradition — and with it a still-salient combination of memories, assumptions, and expectations — upon which the government can construct an effective political case for the maintenance of a significant military capability. By contrast, in the case of Canada, the prevalence of program cuts in other important areas of public policy (health and education among them), when combined with a certain Methodist thrust in the Canadian foreign policy culture, makes this a much harder sell.

The consequences for Canada's capabilities abroad are clear, and in the final session William Hopkinson (ever so gently ... but more than once!) reminded the Colloquium of some of their embarrassing implications for the effectiveness of Canadian diplomacy abroad. His point was reiterated with equal amiability by Bruce George.

This, of course, was the point at which the diplomatic niceties of the occasion gave way for a brief moment to the real differences of circumstance and perspective that confront the two countries. Given the audience, it seems reasonable to conclude that the remonstrations were being delivered, in the main, to the converted. For those on the Canadian side who were defensively inclined, however, it was possible to ask an obvious question: Would Canada's diplomatic influence increase if the defence expenditures went up? On this point, the historical evidence is mixed, which is one of the reasons why sceptics in Canada often seem so hard to convince. Interests, in short, will "out," even among friends.

THE IMMOVABLE OBJECT

On this final matter, there was a certain similarity in the Canadian and UK responses to the American hegemonic fact. It might be possible to sum it up in a simple commandment: "Don't resist. Instead, cozy up, or — occasionally — go around!"

It is possible, although unpopular, to argue that in Canada this commandment represents the single geopolitically driven imperative governing the conduct of Canadian foreign policy. Except for the naïve, the deluded, or the suicidal, obeying it is not a matter of choice. It is a question less of preference, and more of necessity — though the convenience of the first usually helps in practice to conceal the inconvenience of the second.

In the case of the UK, however, there is obviously more room for manoeuvre, much of it now coming from the connection with Europe. The desire to work closely with the United States thus has a more voluntarist flavour in the British context. It is a question less of necessity, and more of preference.

SUMMING IT UP

The foregoing comments could well be regarded as more glibly provocative than finely tuned. Hence, the time has probably come to bring to an end this brief caricature of what was, in fact, a highly sophisticated array of carefully nuanced exchanges. Ending it will also relieve me of the obligation to deal with a seventh theme than ran through at least part of the Colloquium, particularly on the second day. It had to do with the problem of morality and statecraft in general, and with the ethical dilemmas confronting the armaments industry in particular. From so demanding a subject I am delighted to beat a full retreat, leaving the Rights and Wrongs to make their company with Beauty — in the eye of the beholder.

The discussion over the course of the two days was extraordinarily rich, engagingly candid, and impressively detailed. There could be no doubt that "old country" folk and "new country" folk still know how to talk to one another. They do so with an ease, comfort, and mutual understanding of fundamental premises that is rarely replicated in the "transnational" discourse of other populations. It is now often claimed that the objective indicators of the Canada-United Kingdom connection — trade, migration, postsecondary education, and the like — are in decline (if not absolutely, then relatively). That may be. But in the encounters of *cognoscenti*, the conversations are still infused with a sense of the familiar, and with the recognition that both parties are somehow rooted in the same place.

NOTES

An earlier version of this conclusion was published as the rapporteur's report of the Colloquium at which this volume's chapters were first presented. The editors have chosen to leave intact some of the references made in this conclusion, which rather than being devoted to the volume's contents, were reflective of the Colloquium's discussion.

1. Bruce George is a Labour MP and chairman of the House Select Committee on Defence.

Contributors

James Fergusson, Centre for Defence and Security Studies, University of Manitoba

Thierry Gongora, Research Associate, Institut québécois des hautes études internationales, Université Laval

Philip Gummett, Professor of Government and Technology Policy and Pro-Vice Chancellor, University of Manchester

David G. Haglund, Director, Centre for International Relations, Queen's University

Fen Osler Hampson, Professor, The Norman Paterson School of International Affairs, Carleton University

William Hopkinson, Head of the International Security Programme, Royal Institute of International Affairs, London

S. Neil MacFarlane, Lester B. Pearson Professor of International Relations and Director of the Centre for International Studies, University of Oxford

Paul D. Manson, Former Chief of Defence Staff, Ottawa

Rear-Admiral D.E. Miller, Commander Maritime Forces Atlantic, Halifax

Sir Geoffrey Pattie, Marketing Director, GEC plc and Chairman of GEC Marconi, London

Claire Turenne Sjolander, Associate Professor, Political Science and Director, Co-op Programme in Political Science, University of Ottawa

Denis Stairs, McCulloch Professor Department of Political Science, Dalhousie University

Trevor Taylor, Professor and Head of the Department of Defence Management and Security Analysis, Royal Military College of Science, Cranfield University

Queen's Policy Studies
Recent Publications

The Queen's Policy Studies Series is dedicated to the exploration of major policy issues that confront governments in Canada and other western nations. McGill-Queen's University Press is the exclusive world representative and distributor of books in the series.

School of Policy Studies

The Communications Revolution at Work: The Social, Economic and Political Impacts of Technological Change, Robert Boyce (ed.), 1999   Paper ISBN 0-88911-805-1 Cloth 0-88911-807-8

Diplomatic Missions: The Ambassador in Canadian Foreign Policy, Robert Wolfe (ed.), 1998 Paper ISBN 0-88911-801-9 Cloth ISBN 0-88911-803-5

Issues in Defence Management, Douglas L. Bland (ed.), 1998 Paper ISBN 0-88911-809-4 Cloth ISBN 0-88911-811-6

Canada's National Defence, vol. 2, *Defence Organization,* Douglas L. Bland (ed.), 1998 Paper ISBN 0-88911-797-7 Cloth ISBN 0-88911-799-3

Canada's National Defence, vol. 1, *Defence Policy,* Douglas L. Bland (ed.), 1997 Paper ISBN 0-88911-792-6 Cloth ISBN 0-88911-790-X

Lone-Parent Incomes and Social-Policy Outcomes: Canada in International Perspective, Terrance Hunsley, 1997 Paper ISBN 0-88911-751-9 Cloth ISBN 0-88911-757-8

Institute of Intergovernmental Relations

Comparing Federal Systems, 2d ed., Ronald L. Watts, 1999   ISBN 0-88911-835-3

Canada: The State of the Federation 1998/99, vol. 13, *How Canadians Connect,* Harvey Lazar and Tom McIntosh (eds.), 1999   Paper ISBN 0-88911-781-0 Cloth ISBN 0-88911-779-9

Canada: The State of the Federation 1997, vol. 12, *Non-Constitutional Renewal,* Harvey Lazar (ed.), 1998 Paper ISBN 0-88911-765-9 Cloth ISBN 0-88911-767-5

Canadian Constitutional Dilemmas Revisited, Denis Magnusson (ed.), 1997 Paper ISBN 0-88911-593-1 Cloth ISBN 0-88911-595-8

Canada: The State of the Federation 1996, Patrick C. Fafard and Douglas M. Brown (eds.), 1997 Paper ISBN 0-88911-587-7 Cloth ISBN 0-88911-597-4

John Deutsch Institute for the Study of Economic Policy

Room to Manoeuvre? Globalization and Policy Convergence, Thomas J. Courchene (ed.), Bell Canada Papers no. 6, 1999   Paper ISBN 0-88911-812-4 Cloth ISBN 0-88911-812-4

Women and Work, Richard P. Chaykowski and Lisa M. Powell (eds.), 1999 Paper ISBN 0-88911-808-6 Cloth ISBN 0-88911-806-X

Equalization: Its Contribution to Canada's Economic and Fiscal Progress, Robin W. Boadway and Paul A.R. Hobson (eds.), Policy Forum Series no. 36, 1998 Paper ISBN 0-88911-780-2 Cloth IBSN 0-88911-804-3

Fiscal Targets and Economic Growth, Thomas J. Courchene and Thomas A. Wilson (eds.), Roundtable Series no. 12, 1998   Paper ISBN 0-88911-778-0 Cloth ISBN 0-88911-776-4

The 1997 Federal Budget: Retrospect and Prospect, Thomas J. Courchene and Thomas A. Wilson (eds.), Policy Forum Series no. 35, 1997   Paper ISBN 0-88911-774-8 Cloth ISBN 0-88911-772-1

Available from:
McGill-Queen's University Press
Tel: 1-800-387-0141 (ON and QC excluding Northwestern ON)
        1-800-387-0172 (all other provinces and Northwestern ON)

E-mail: customer.service@ccmailgw.genpub.com